About t

Sally Welch is Spirituality Ad
She leads the family and cl
Oxford, where these craft activities are trialled. She also
leads training events for the Diocese of Oxford in the area of
spirituality and is Diocesan Labyrinth Coordinator.

Her published works are: *Making a Pilgrimage* (Lion
Hudson, 2009), *Walking the Labyrinth* (Canterbury Press,
2010), *Every Place is Holy Ground* (Canterbury Press, 2011)
and *Edible Bible Crafts* (Barnabas for Children, 2014). She is
also a contributor to BRF's spirituality resource *Quiet Spaces*.

Barnabas
for
Children®

Barnabas for Children® is a registered word mark and the logo is a registered device mark of
The Bible Reading Fellowship.

Text copyright © Sally Welch 2014
The author asserts the moral right
to be identified as the author of this work

Published by
The Bible Reading Fellowship
15 The Chambers, Vineyard
Abingdon, OX14 3FE, United Kingdom
Tel: +44 (0)1865 319700
Email: enquiries@brf.org.uk
Website: www.brf.org.uk
BRF is a Registered Charity

ISBN 978 1 84101 711 2
First published 2014
10 9 8 7 6 5 4 3 2 1 0

Acknowledgements
Unless otherwise stated, scripture quotations are taken from The New Revised Standard
Version of the Bible, Anglicised Edition, copyright © 1989, 1995 by the Division of Christian
Education of the National Council of the Churches of Christ in the USA, are used by
permission. All rights reserved.

Scripture quotations taken from The Holy Bible, New International Version (Anglicised edition)
copyright © 1973, 1978, 1984, 2011 by Biblica (formerly International Bible Society). Used
by permission of Hodder & Stoughton Publishers, an Hachette UK company. All rights
reserved. 'NIV' is a registered trade mark of Biblica (formerly International Bible Society). UK
trademark number 1448790.

Extracts from the Authorised Version of the Bible (The King James Bible), the rights in which
are vested in the Crown, are reproduced by permission of the Crown's patentee, Cambridge
University Press.

Unless otherwise stated, Bible story extracts are taken from *The Barnabas Children's Bible* by
Rhona Davies (Barnabas for Children, 2012), used by permission.

Cover photo: © Aleksandr Glushkov/Agasfer/iStock/Thinkstock; girl in church © ronhall/
iStock/Thinkstock; craft photos © Sally Welch

Every effort has been made to trace and contact copyright owners for material used in this
resource. We apologise for any inadvertent omissions or errors, and would ask those concerned
to contact us so that full acknowledgment can be made in the future.

A catalogue record for this book is available from the British Library

Printed and bound by CPI Group (UK) Ltd, Croydon CR0 4YY

Celebrating Festivals

Readings, reflections, crafts and prayer
activities for 20 major church festivals

Sally Welch

To Liz, without whom this book would not have been possible, and Binka, who patiently tested all the crafts.

Acknowledgements

With thanks to Andrew Bunch and the community of St Margaret's Church, Oxford

Unless otherwise stated, Bible story extracts are taken from *The Barnabas Children's Bible* by Rhona Davies (Barnabas for Children, 2012).

Contents

6

Introduction

The importance of place

This section is not intended to be an in-depth study of sacred space but is simply a description of the principles that lie behind the prayers and activities suggested in this book. It is a reflection drawn from many years in different church buildings, observing a wide variety of people as they engage with the space that is contained within the church building.

For centuries the church building stood firmly in the centre of its community, the largest and grandest of the buildings, with only the home of the Lord of the Manor even approaching it for size and wealth. Even today, although in many towns and cities huge edifices of glass and steel have eclipsed the local church, still it stands, solid and unchanging, as a symbol of God's presence in and love for the community that surrounds it. By Christians the church can be seen as a statement of belief in a world of non-belief, a reminder of another kingdom, with different values, stretching beyond our world out into eternity. By other inhabitants it is seen as a witness to the faith of others, perhaps never needed but available if called upon.

The building can be a reminder of the many people who have prayed there, of the significant moments in the lives of individuals and communities that have been celebrated there. The space becomes the holder of a community's story, and of the stories of the individuals whose births, marriages and deaths have been ritualised within its walls.

More important than this, however, is the invitation that a church offers to engage with the sacredness of the place, and use it to encounter God and to make meaning from our life experiences. We are invited, once within the walls of the church, to make time for the transcendent, to look further than ourselves and our personal concerns to the world beyond and the kingdom beyond that. It is a place for realigning ourselves with the divine, for reconnecting with the love of God, for rebuilding relationships with Christ and, through him, with each other. Even the objects within a church, the pulpit, the font, the chairs themselves, can help us to recall our identities as children of God and our relationship with his world.

A church, in the final analysis, is indeed the community of Christ, the worshipping congregation, and any importance ascribed to a church building must always come a good second to that of the living souls within it. However, a space that is set aside, encouraging reflection and prayer and an encounter with the sacred, has a value that must not be denied.

Sacred space and children

The layout of the church, its state of tidiness and the nature of its displays, say a great deal about the priorities of its congregation. Some churches have dedicated a significant part of a side chapel or nave to a massive organ, others have extended the kitchen and hospitality area so that it takes over one-third of the available space. Some notice boards abound in legal notices and electoral roll information; others are given over to displays from the various charities supported by the church. For this reason, it is always interesting to see what sort of accommodation has been provided for the younger age groups in a church community. Some churches have set aside entire rooms for the use of children and teenagers, with vibrant displays and casual seating. Others have worked hard at setting up sacred spaces that appeal particularly to young spiritualities, with objects and pictures and brightly coloured lettering. In many churches, however, it would be very difficult indeed to judge whether any children attended the church, so little evidence is there of their existence. And yet children too are alive to the numinous, the transcendent, perhaps in a way more aware of its possibilities than adults whose sensibilities have been hardened by a prolonged interaction with the secular world. The church building and the furniture within it can provide a springboard for exploration of individual spirituality and corporate belief.

On a very basic level, the church building is a wonderful place for children to explore, encouraging a reaching out beyond the familiar confines of home and school to a building that in its very nature is strange and unfamiliar. Its size enables children to play at some distance from parents yet still remain safe. The objects often contained within it—stone steps, marble floors, high wooden pews—are sufficiently hazardous to provoke excitement, and flexible enough to enable all sorts of games to take place. With encouragement and just the right amount of adult engagement, these games can lead to thoughts on the sacred dimension of the objects: travelling from font to altar can remind us of the journey of Mary and Joseph to Bethlehem, climbing stairs encourages stories of Moses receiving the ten commandments, chasing games of the adventures of Joseph in Egypt.

More proactive engagement with the church building through activities such as those described in this book can have a twofold benefit. They enable children to become familiar not only with the stories of our faith, but also with the festivals that mark out the church calendar and with the objects that Christians hold as significant and special. Establishing relationships between stories and objects reinforces an appreciation of both, bringing a potentially dull object such as a stone font alive and revealing its wider meaning and purpose, and also earthing the stories that are the foundation of belief in something real and physical, making connections between them and our material world.

In addition to this is the effect of the events on the rest of the church community. Not every member of the congregation will be able to be a volunteer, but all can get involved with the provision of raw materials such as cardboard tubes or margarine tubs. Every festival contains one craft activity that can be worked on by a group of children together. This should, if possible, be displayed in the church as a reminder that children too are members of the community and are walking the same path as even the most elderly worshipper.

Early encounters and familiarity with the church building can leave the doors open to future encounters. Even if there is no subsequent engagement with church beyond activity mornings, this should not engender a sense of failure from the organisers of such events. Embedded within the subconscious will be an awareness of a place of safety, of community, of purposefully seeking a meaning beyond the consumerism and haste of contemporary society. This may lead to the desire in later life to explore the faith that lies behind such a place, or simply remain as the knowledge that such a place exists in this world.

The practicalities

*

Suggestions for organising crafts for young children

General safety

Inevitably, crafting activities involve some safety hazards, and it is the responsibility of the organisers to minimise these. Food safety and hygiene is covered in more depth below, but in addition to these, adults should ensure that sharp knives and scissors are never left lying around, and that any crafts using small objects that could be a choking hazard are continually supervised by adults. Try to keep the ratio of adults to children as high as possible on tables where there are buttons, sequins and other small decorative objects. Children's scissors should always be used, rather than sharp pointed ones, and ordinary dinner knives will serve their purpose of cutting or spreading for all crafts.

Food safety

When setting up edible craft sessions for children, hygiene and food safety is an absolute priority.

None of the recipes in this book contains nuts because these can produce the most violent allergic reactions (see p. 14, 'Allergies and food intolerances'). They do not use raw egg or any food product that needs to be kept refrigerated at all times. If your craft sessions are taking place in a cold church building, the ambient room temperature will probably not be so high that special precautions are necessary to keep food cool. However, if your room is warm, take care not to bring out ingredients such as cheese or eggs until just before the start of the craft session.

None of the recipes uses food that has to be hot, so there should be no risk of burns or scalds.

Make sure that you have wiped every surface with antibacterial spray before setting up the craft. The best method is to cover your tables with banqueting paper, such as the sort used in industrial catering. This way, you can ensure that the surface is perfectly clean and also keep the clearing up to a minimum.

On every table, keep a supply of antibacterial wet wipes and encourage the children to use them frequently to wipe fingers and hands. Strongly discourage the licking of fingers, and even more strongly discourage the unconscious tendency for writing icing tubes, icing knives and other implements to find their way into toddlers' mouths.

There should also be a bottle of antibacterial hand cleanser on every table. Every child should use it at the beginning of the session and again every time they return to the edible craft table, having been away from it for however short a time. At the end of the session, children should be encouraged to clean their hands again with the hand cleanser.

Food crafting equipment should be kept separately from other craft supplies. Scissors and knives should be bought and used only for food and stored in airtight boxes. Other equipment should be safely stored in airtight containers.

Allergies and food intolerance

Many children suffer from one of a range of food allergies and intolerances, and one danger when working with very young children and food is that these allergies may not yet have manifested themselves. Nuts can provoke particularly severe reactions, so there are no nuts or nut products used in any of these recipes.

When baking for the edible crafts, take care that the kitchen is entirely clear of nuts or nut products, as even using a chopping board that has been previously used for nuts can provoke a reaction.

Other allergens, such as wheat and egg, can be avoided either by using the gluten- and egg-free recipes or by using an alternative, such as rice cakes or biscuits, instead of cakes.

When working with children who have a known food allergy, great care must be taken to avoid cross-contamination—for example, knives being used to cut cakes and then spread icing on biscuits. If a child has a particularly severe allergy, it might be best to ensure that the entire craft is free from the allergen, rather than restricting the child to a particular part of the craft or placing them on a separate table.

Setting up and clearing up

The most important thing to remember when setting up is to make the area look both clean and inviting. This does not mean buying expensive furniture or equipment, but it may mean rearranging the resources you have and covering as much as possible in bright tablecloths. Paper tablecloths can be bought quite cheaply at supermarkets and party shops. However, a general call to the congregation will usually produce many unused fabric tablecloths from former days of tea parties and formal dining.

It is worth trying to provide some sort of protective clothing, such as old shirts, if possible.

To create the crafting area, begin by clearing away as much furniture as possible. The children will need space to craft and the adults will need a good line of sight to see what is going on. Arrange tables and chairs so that there is space for adult helpers as well as children, making sure that the furniture you use can be easily wiped clean. If possible, cover the tables with disposable table cloths or banqueting roll; this makes clearing up much quicker and avoids the hygiene issues that come with working in church buildings.

If there are not enough tables and chairs, cover a large area of floor with tablecloths or banqueting roll and encourage the children to stay seated while they are crafting.

If you are doing one of the group messy crafts, allow plenty of space for the children to come and go. If possible, keep this craft area a little separate from the others, to enable children to move around freely. If you are having messy crafts and edible crafts at the same time, try to keep the two areas as separate as possible. If the craft involves finger paints or hand prints, make sure there is somewhere for children to wash before they move on to the edible crafts.

In the middle of the tables, place a supply of antibacterial wipes and a bottle of antibacterial hand cleanser.

Lay the crafting ingredients out on the table before the activity begins; it makes matters much more complicated and dangerous if people are carrying trays and jars around young children. If the food is in danger of becoming too warm or too cold, bring it out at the last minute.

Arrange the crafting ingredients so that they can be easily seen, with the same types of ingredients together. Always make a prototype so that the children and their helpers can see what is to be made. If the craft is complicated, you may want to provide two or three examples at different stages of crafting.

Clearing up is most quickly done by a group of adults while the children are occupied with another activity. However, children can learn much by helping to tidy up, and sharing cleaning tasks can become part of the crafting activity. Do not move tables and chairs while young children are present, however, as the safety issues are too serious.

Basic equipment for messy crafts

Although some of the crafts will need additional items specific to the craft, such as margarine pots or balloons, the following is a list of things of which you should have a supply. They are all readily obtainable, in large supermarkets or pound shops or in craft supply shops such as Hobbycraft.

- Glue gun
- Washable PVA glue
- Masking tape
- Sticky tape
- Double-sided tape
- Acrylic paint in all colours
- Poster paint in all colours
- Paint brushes, both thick and thin
- Lining paper, found in DIY shops—this is a very cheap

way of providing paper for large-scale craft projects
- Thin card in all colours, including silver and gold. If you buy photocopiable card, that will save time if you want to print templates from the internet
- Tissue paper in all colours
- Paper in all colours and patterns
- Pencils
- Felt pens or crayons
- Children's safety scissors
- Glitter
- A selection of sequins, buttons, feathers and other decorations. I usually buy any that are on special offer. The self-adhesive variety is always best—glueing on sequins is messy and they take a while to dry
- Large and small craft sticks
- Self-adhesive 'wobbly' eyes in various sizes
- Dolly pegs
- Scraps of felt and fabric; ask the congregation for offcuts of fabric and embroidery materials
- Silver foil
- Drinking straws

Basic equipment for edible crafts

- Cake rack for cooling cakes—buy enough racks to cool a batch of cakes. If you are cooking 36 cakes at a time, you will need two or three racks.
- Cake tins for small and medium size fairy cakes. The tins do not have to be expensive; the cheapest ones your supermarket can provide are absolutely fine. Buy as many as you have shelves in your oven as that way you can be

economical with your electricity and cook 24 or 36 cakes at a time.

- Paper cake cases. I have found that the very cheap cases come away from the cake mixture during the cooking process and look rather untidy at the end. It is better to opt for a mid-range, such as made by Dr Oetker, which are widely available. Don't buy large or muffin cases as they either use too much batter or look half empty when they are cooked.
- A sharp knife
- Electric mixer or food blender. While not absolutely necessary, they will save you a lot of hard work. Again, these do not have to be expensive. I use a supermarket 'value' electric mixer and it is absolutely fine.
- Baking parchment—a vital piece of kitchen equipment for rolling out biscuit dough, fondant icing and so on. Buy in large quantities as you will need a lot!
- Rolling pin

Basic equipment for crafting

Don't worry if you do not have enough for each child—part of the learning process for these crafts is to be found in the idea of sharing equipment and taking turns.

- Blunt-ended knives
- Flower-shaped cookie cutters in at least two sizes
- Cross-shaped cookie cutter
- Piping bags and icing nozzles of various sizes
- Children's rolling pins

Basic ingredients for edible crafts

All the basic ingredients can be bought in a supermarket. You may have to go to a larger store for the toppings or additional ingredients, but nothing requires a specialist shop.

Savoury crafts

For the bases, you will need:

- tortillas
- rice cakes
- bagels
- bread rolls
- rice

The most commonly used toppings are:

- slices of processed cheese
- 'spaghetti' cheese
- Parmesan cheese
- 'squirty' cheese
- Small round cheeses
- vegetables that can be eaten raw, such as carrots, cucumber, peppers, celery, mangetout, lettuce, broccoli
- black olives
- mayonnaise, ideally in a bottle
- straight pretzels
- Twiglets®
- tortilla chips

Sweet crafts

You will need the following ingredients for fairy cakes and biscuits:

- plain flour
- self-raising flour
- baking powder
- eggs
- caster sugar
- butter or margarine

You can use the cheapest brand of margarine available, but this can be quite gritty and your cakes may not rise as well. Certainly the biscuits will not taste as good. I tend to use a branded cooking margarine for cakes but prefer the cheapest unsalted butter for biscuits. They are much easier to make with butter, saving you valuable time, and the end result is very tasty.

Toppings

The most commonly used toppings are:

- mini Smarties®
- Oreo® cookies
- marshmallows, big and small
- wafer biscuits
- fig rolls
- digestive biscuits

- syrup pancakes
- icing sugar (if you are going to make your own buttercream icing)

Decorating essentials

- Sugar balls and sprinkles

Fondant icing

This is the icing most commonly used in the recipes. It is easy to roll out and mould and is not too expensive. You can buy large blocks of white fondant in most supermarkets, and many shops also stock smaller boxes of fondant in five basic colours. Small amounts of different colours can be made using white icing and food colouring. Use only the smallest amount of food colouring: a little goes a long way. It will take a while to knead in so that the colour is spread evenly. If the icing warms up too much in your hands, it will get sticky; if so, just put it in the fridge for five minutes.

For crafts using larger amounts of pink, for example, it is much easier to buy ready-coloured icing from somewhere like Hobbycraft or your local cake decorating shop.

Fondant icing can be rolled out easily, especially if you sandwich it between two pieces of baking parchment while rolling. One way to prevent it sticking is to sprinkle it with icing sugar, but this can make the icing dry out too quickly.

If crafting with children under ten, it is really worth cutting out flat shapes, such as circles to go on top of fairy cakes, beforehand. Sprinkled with icing sugar and kept under clingfilm, they will last a day or two before getting too brittle. Moulding is another matter: the icing can be treated like modelling clay and shaped accordingly.

Fondant icing, once opened, must be stored carefully. Wrap it up in many layers of clingfilm so that it is airtight, or it will be dry and unusable.

Buttercream icing

You can make buttercream icing easily, but be aware that if you use the cheaper sort of margarine to do so, that will be evident in the taste. It really is best to use real, unsalted butter: the cheapest is fine. A quicker alternative is to buy the pots of ready-made buttercream icing that are available in many supermarkets. Once opened, these can be stored in the fridge for quite a long time.

To make buttercream icing, you need to use butter at room temperature, or the process will take much too long. Once your butter is at the right temperature, simply use twice the weight of sifted icing sugar to butter and mix thoroughly. If the icing is too stiff, you can add a drop of water; if too runny, add more icing sugar. Add vanilla or cocoa to make the variations specified in the craft ingredients lists.

Writing icing

You can make writing icing by mixing a small amount of water with icing sugar until you get the consistency you require; then use an icing bag with a fine nozzle. In my experience, this will prove quite messy and difficult to handle for smaller children. By far the best option is to buy little tubes of ready-made writing icing, available from supermarkets and cake decorating shops. The larger tubes are more problematic, as the icing needs to be quite stiff to pipe and the tubes are often too hard to squash for small hands.

Food colourings

It is worth splashing out on the professional food colourings that you can buy in small jars, rather than the bottles of liquid colouring usually found in supermarkets. These have a tendency to make everything runnier and harder to manage. The professional varieties are more solid and, although expensive, last a long time.

*

Resources

Where to shop for messy crafts

Most of the skill in shopping for craft materials lies in buying interesting stuff when you see it. Wander into pound shops, and shops that take up end of leases, and have a look in the local market for things like clothes pegs that are on special offer. Even if you cannot see a use for it at the time, there will be occasions when you can extract exactly what you need from the craft cupboard. Apart from items bought at regular trips to places such as these, all of the materials needed for the crafts in this book can be purchased easily either in specialist craft shops such as Hobbycraft or online from places such as Baker Ross or Yellow Moon.

Do not underestimate your church congregation as a supplier of craft materials either. A call for empty loo rolls to our local church produced hundreds; in fact, so many that we had to follow up with a plea to stop giving loo rolls! Congregations can supply empty margarine tubs, tin cans, scraps of fabric and yarn, old shirts for overalls or large pieces of cardboard for group artwork. Once you have engaged their imaginations, there will be no end to what they can provide.

Where to shop for edible crafts

As with the messy crafts, most of the edible ingredients in this book can be purchased in ordinary supermarkets. Ethically-aware shoppers will find that the Fairtrade range carried by most supermarkets will cover most ingredients, except for the decorating items, such as writing icing. Where possible, home-made alternatives have been suggested.

The baking and decorating equipment has, similarly, been kept as simple as possible. However, if you are stocking up for the first time, it might be a good idea either to visit some large craft shops or to look online. Hobbycraft and Lakeland both stock a wide range of cake-making and decorating equipment, which can be bought fairly cheaply, as long as the temptation to add extra interesting things to the list is resisted.

Preparation in advance

Most of the recipes in this book have been used for crafting sessions involving up to 50 children, the oldest of whom is about ten years old and the youngest one year old. With such large numbers and wide age range, I have learnt that it is best to do as much of the preparation in advance as possible. Although parents are encouraged to join in the crafting sessions, those with more than one child cannot watch them all, and it can be quite frustrating to be struggling to roll out fondant icing, especially if there is a queue for the rolling pin. Equally, some parents of young children may not have encountered crafts before. Every effort should be made to encourage them to craft alongside their children rather than having both parent and child waiting helplessly for help and instruction.

For these reasons, where suggestions have been made for preparation, they have come from hard-earned experience of the capabilities of such a group. If your group is smaller or your children are older, preparation in advance can be put aside.

Remember, however, that any craft involving cooking or use of the glue gun, sharp knives or scissors or other hazardous equipment, must be done by adults in advance.

*

Recipes and techniques

These recipes all work well with gluten-free flour.

Fairy cakes

The simplest and quickest way to provide fairy cakes for a large number of people is probably to go to a large supermarket and buy them! Twelve fairy cakes can cost less than £1 and, if you have no time or equipment for mass production, this is the easiest solution. However, cakes are not difficult to make at home and it only takes about 15 minutes to produce as many as you have oven space to cook. This recipe is practically foolproof and can be multiplied up according to how many cakes you want to make.

Before you begin, it is a good idea to make sure that your oven is level on the floor, otherwise you will produce uneven cakes as the mixture slips to one side in the cooking process. It is also worth working out which way up your oven shelves go: one way is often more level than another. This sounds a bit over-conscientious, but level fairy cakes are easier to decorate.

Ingredients

- 120 g self-raising flour
- 120 g margarine
- 120 g caster sugar

- 2 eggs
- 1 tsp of baking powder

These quantities make about 18 small fairy cakes.

1. Turn the oven to 180°C/Gas Mark 4 to pre-heat while you prepare the mixture.
2. Line two 12-hole cake tins with paper cake cases.
3. Weigh all the ingredients into a large mixing bowl and beat with an electric whisk. You can do this by hand, but it will take a long time and make your arm ache. The mixture will gradually turn a paler colour and become light and fluffy.
4. Check the consistency of the mixture. If you lift a spoonful of it out of the bowl, it should drop off the spoon slowly.
5. Put about a teaspoonful of cake mixture into each paper cake case. Only trial and error will help you discover how much to put in each case. If you want cakes of an equal size, you can pipe the mixture in using an icing bag, but this is time-consuming and not really necessary. After all, once the icing is on, little of the cake will be seen.
6. Place the cakes in the oven for about 8 minutes. This is usually just long enough to wash up your cooking equipment, but if you use a timer you will get a more consistent result. If your oven cooks unevenly, open the door after about 6 minutes and turn the trays round.
7. Check after 8 minutes to see if the cakes look light brown in colour. Test them by pushing down gently with your finger on top of a cake. If it springs back and is firm to the touch, then the cakes are cooked. Here again, trial and error will help you discover how long the cakes need.

8. Once the cakes are cooked, take them out of the tins and let them cool on a wire rack.

Variations

For most crafts, it is best to stick to ordinary fairy cakes, as, once you are familiar with the recipe, they will become very quick and easy to make. However, you could try the following if you want a change.

- Chocolate fairy cakes: swap 20 g cocoa (not drinking chocolate) for 20 g flour.
- Sultana fairy cakes: stir in 20 g sultanas just before the mixture goes in the cases.

Biscuits

These biscuits are very quick and easy to make, as you can use an electric beater rather than crumbling the mixture with your fingers first. Make sure that the butter is at room temperature, though, or it will be very hard work. Once again, you can use margarine instead of butter, but the taste will be poorer. It depends on whether you think people will actually notice what the end product tastes like or whether the joy really lies in the crafting.

Ingredients

- 200 g unsalted butter
- 200 g caster sugar

- 1 beaten egg
- 400 g flour

1. Turn the oven to 180°C/Gas Mark 4 to pre-heat while you prepare the mixture.
2. Beat the sugar and butter together until they lighten in colour and become smooth.
3. Gradually add the egg, beating all the time.
4. Add the flour, beating slowly until the ingredients start to come together into a lump.
5. Bring the dough together into a ball with your hands, then wrap it in clingfilm and put it in the fridge for 10 minutes. Do not be tempted to shortcut this stage, as the chilling process makes the dough much easier to roll out. Similarly, if you make the dough the day before, take it out of the fridge half an hour before you need to roll it or it will crumble.
6. Roll out the dough between two sheets of baking paper. This will stop it sticking to the rolling pin or the work surface and makes rolling much easier.
7. Cut out your shapes and place them on lightly greased baking trays, then put them back in the fridge for another 10 minutes. If you are in a hurry, you can skip this step, but the biscuits cook better from chilled.
8. Cook for about 8 minutes or until light brown. Don't let them get too dark as they will continue cooking on the tray for a few minutes after you have taken them out of the oven.
9. Once the biscuits are cooked, keep them on the tray to harden for a minute or so, then transfer them to a wire rack to cool.

Scones

Ingredients

- 225 g self-raising flour
- 55 g butter or margarine
- 150 g milk
- Baking sheet
- Circular cookie cutter

1. Pre-heat the oven to 200°C/Gas Mark 6.
2. Chop the butter or margarine into small pieces and place in a large mixing bowl.
3. Add the flour, then rub between your fingers until the mixture looks like fine bread crumbs.
4. Pour in the milk and stir with a flat-bladed knife until the mixture starts to form a dough.
5. Bring together with your hands and knead briefly until you have a smooth dough.
6. Wrap the dough in clingfilm and chill for 20 minutes.
7. Roll out the dough between two sheets of baking paper until it is about 3 cm thick. Try to roll out the dough as gently and smoothly as possible so that it rises evenly.
8. Cut out circles using a cutter and place on a greased baking sheet.
9. Bake for 10 minutes or until light brown and well risen.

Icing

Much has been written about the techniques of icing and decorating cakes, none of which will be needed for these recipes. All you need is an ordinary kitchen knife for spreading icing. Occasionally a steady hand will be needed—for example, if only part of a cake surface is to be covered in a particular colour.

Melting chocolate

You can melt chocolate on a stove by breaking it into small pieces and putting it in a bowl over a saucepan of gently simmering water, without allowing the water to touch the bottom of the bowl. Be very careful not to let even a drop of water get into the bowl, or the chocolate will become gritty and unusable. It is easier to use a microwave, if you have one: simply break the pieces into a bowl and microwave on medium in 30-second bursts, stopping to stir the chocolate until it is melted.

You cannot melt white chocolate or food colouring. If you want coloured chocolate, you can buy coloured chocolate or candy buttons for melting from Hobbycraft, Lakeland or other cake decorating shops.

The festivals

*

Advent Sunday

Theme: getting ready

Place/object within the church building: vestry

Suggested Bible passages

Old Testament: Genesis 18:1–14

Is anything too wonderful for the Lord? At the set time I will return to you, in due season, and Sarah shall have a son.
GENESIS 18:14

New Testament: Luke 1:26–38

Then Mary said, 'Here am I, the servant of the Lord; let it be with me according to your word.'
LUKE 1:38A

Reflection for leaders

I have only once been in a vestry that was immaculately tidy, and that was in the chapel of an Oxford college, presided over by a musical director who had a fierce and proprietorial attitude to the entire chapel, focusing on the vestry as a place where absolutely everything had its place and no disorder was allowed. This was the exception, however, to the large number of vestries I have been in where the mess ranged from the mildly disorganised to the totally catastrophic. To a large extent, this is how it should be. After all, the vestry is the place where the leaders of the worshipping community get ready, and there will always be a certain amount of confusion and activity around that process.

The vestry may appear to be merely a small, untidy room where everything is put to get it out of the way, including, sometimes, the Sunday school, but its symbolic role is much greater than that. For the vestry is a transitional place, a 'quasi-liminal' area, where preparations are made for the main event that happens in the church. Often, the worship leaders prepare themselves here and the choir pauses here for prayer before beginning the procession into church, and repeats the action after the service. It is here that members of the church, often including children, act as a community on the threshold of the reality of the worshipping action. The anthropologist Van Gennep wrote of people in liminal places as being in transition: 'Whoever passes from one to the other finds himself physically and magico-religiously in a special situation for a certain length of time: he wavers between two worlds' (*Rites of Passage*, Routledge Kegan Paul, 1960). In the vestry we are between the outside world and the worshipping church; people discover one another on a different level, and an intense community spirit, a feeling of great social equality, solidarity and togetherness can be formed.

The season of Advent is a time of preparation, of getting ready. There will be some confusion as to its purpose: are we rehearsing carols or engaging in a time of repentance, decorating the church or stripping it bare prior to the celebration of the Saviour's birth? This is only to be expected, for that very first Advent must have been approached with the same mixed feelings by Mary and Joseph. Mary had said 'yes' to God's great plan; she had offered up her whole life to him ('Let it be to me according to your word') but she must have wondered what on earth she had let herself in for. Joseph, too, had debated hard over his future course of action when he was told of Mary's pregnancy; he knew difficult times lay ahead. They were also preparing for a new and intimate experience of God's love, not just for them as individuals but for the whole world. So the vestry stands for us as a symbol of Advent, of waiting, of preparing and getting ready, both physically and spiritually. We are apprehensive about the demands that saying 'yes' to the love of God will make upon us, but we are also alive with excitement as a community prepares to rejoice at the birth of new hope, the redemption of a promise, the gift of new life.

Bible story

The angel Gabriel went to see Mary, who lived in Nazareth in Galilee. Mary was not much more than a girl but she was engaged to be married to Joseph, the local carpenter.

'Mary,' said Gabriel. 'God is with you!'

Mary was afraid. She didn't know what to think.

'There is no need to be afraid!' said Gabriel. 'You will bear a son and give him the name Jesus. He will be known as God's son and will be a king who will reign for ever!'

'But I am not yet married,' said Mary. 'How can I have a baby?'

'The Holy Spirit will make this happen, for God is able to do anything. Another woman in your family, Elizabeth, is now six months' pregnant. Everyone said that she couldn't have children, but with God, nothing is impossible.'

'I will do anything God wants me to,' said Mary. 'I am ready to serve him in this way.'

Then Gabriel left Mary.

'I wonder...'

I wonder what the angel looked like...
I wonder what Mary felt when she heard what the angel said...
I wonder what Mary said to Joseph about her news...
I wonder what Joseph thought...
I wonder how I can get ready for Christmas...

Prayer activity

You will need:
- An empty manger, in proportion to the size of your prayer group (for half a dozen or fewer, use a large margarine tub, covered with brown paper and decorated to look like strips of wood; for a larger group, use a cardboard box or, better still, a wooden orange box)
- Straw-coloured paper
- Paper shredder (if not available, several pairs of scissors will be fine)
- Doll of an appropriate size, wrapped in a white blanket to go in the manger on Christmas Day

If there is room for your group to go into the vestry, take them in there. Discuss the sorts of things that happen in a vestry, and explain that it is a room for getting ready in. If the Sunday school happens in there, ask how a Sunday school helps them to get ready. Remind the children that Advent is a time for getting ourselves, and our world, ready to celebrate Jesus' birth, and ask them what that might involve. You can steer the conversation away from buying presents, perhaps, to tidying up the house for Christmas visitors. This can lead on to a discussion about how we can get ourselves ready, by tidying away things we do that are unkind or unhelpful, which would not be welcoming to a new baby. Ask the children to write or draw one or more of these things.

Remind the children that Jesus' birth heralds the approach of the kingdom of God, and ask them what sort of a world that might be. What sort of things would happen in a new world? What sort of things would not?

Ask the children to write or draw their dreams for the world, or for the new baby, on the sheets of paper.

Gather the sheets of paper together and then either shred them or cut them into long strips. Explain that these hopes and dreams and prayers will be the straw for the baby Jesus' bed and that on Christmas Day you will put in a doll as the baby, who will be made comfortable by their thoughts and prayers.

Spend a few moments in silence looking at the manger and thinking about their hopes for the future.

Craft activities

Advent wreath

You will need:
- Thick paper or thin card, in green
- Oasis ring
- 4 red candles (optional: plus a white one)
- Branches of fir and holly, cut into child-friendly pieces
- Cardboard ring that will fit snugly round the outside of the oasis ring
- Glitter, pencils, scissors

First of all, ask the children to draw round the outline of their outstretched hands on green paper or card, and cut it out. You can get young children to do a green handprint that can be cut out by adults, if this is easier.

Decorate the handprints with glitter.

While the handprints are drying, construct the inner Advent wreath. Start by putting the four red candles into the oasis ring to represent the four weeks of Advent. If there is a place for a final white candle in the centre, to be lit on Christmas Day, that is excellent, but the wreath is fine without one.

Poke the pieces of fir and holly into the oasis ring until it is completely covered.

Glue the hands on to the cardboard ring, which will make the outer wreath, with the palms facing inwards towards the centre. Put the outer ring round the inner ring.

Place the wreath on a table out of reach of small children,

and light one candle for each week of Advent, until all four are lit on the last Sunday in Advent.

Empty stable

You will need:
- 6 large craft sticks
- 2 smaller craft sticks
- 1 A4 piece of stiff card
- Strong glue
- Scraps of fabric, felt, paper or similar
- Paint or felt-tip pens
- Scissors

First, cut three of the large craft sticks and both of the smaller craft sticks in half. You might need to do this beforehand. It can be done with strong scissors but is quite difficult.

The craft sticks can be coloured or painted brown to look like wood.

On to the stiff card, make the outline of a stable using the large craft sticks. One stick laid horizontally is the floor of the stable, with the two half sticks vertically at either end to form the walls. The roof is made by two craft sticks sloped together to form a pointed roof.

Two small half craft sticks should be glued together to form an uneven X-shape, with the bottom half of the X being shorter than the top. This will be the manger. Glue it into the stable, then glue some scraps of paper or hay in the top half of the X.

The three large half sticks will be Mary, Joseph and the angel. Colour or decorate these using scraps of fabric or felt or coloured paper.

Place Mary and Joseph on either side of the manger, and the angel on the roof.

Baby Jesus is made from a small half craft stick. He can go in the manger on Christmas Day, or sooner if you are worried he might get lost.

Edible craft activities

Savoury bagel wreath

You will need (per wreath):
- Half a bagel, sliced horizontally
- Mayonnaise for spreading
- 5 cherry tomatoes
- Small lettuce leaves, the smaller the better
- A few slices of red pepper
- Small star cutter

Spread the bagel with mayonnaise.

Arrange the lettuce leaves on the bagel to look like holly leaves.

Chop the cherry tomatoes in half.

Arrange the cherry tomatoes on the lettuce leaves to look like holly berries.

Slice some thin slices of red pepper and arrange to look like a bow at the top of the bagel.

Sweet Rice Krispies® wreath

You will need (makes about 12 wreaths, depending on size):
- 90 g Rice Krispies® or cornflakes
- 4 tbsp of golden syrup
- 15 g sugar
- 15 g butter
- Green fondant icing
- Red sugar balls or red writing icing

Melt the butter, golden syrup and sugar gently together over a low heat. When the mixture is melted, pour in the Rice Krispies and stir until they are all coated.

Working with a spoonful of the mixture you have created at a time, make a wreath shape on some baking paper and leave to set.

While this is setting, make holly leaves with the green fondant icing, either using a small cutter or cutting them freehand. Stick the leaves in place on the wreath with the writing icing. Decorate with sugar balls or red writing icing for berries.

You can use marshmallows instead of the golden syrup and sugar, but I find this mixture, although it sets satisfyingly hard, incredibly sticky to work with, and you end up with more on your hands than on the baking sheet!

A quicker alternative is to use Rice Krispies Squares, and cut out a wreath shape using two sizes of circle cutter.

*

Christmas

Theme: Jesus' birth gives all children value

Place/object within the church building: children's corner

Suggested Bible passages

Old Testament: Isaiah 52:7–9

How beautiful upon the mountains are the feet of the messenger who announces peace.
ISAIAH 52:7

New Testament: Luke 2:1–7

And she gave birth to her firstborn son and wrapped him in bands of cloth and laid him in a manger, because there was no place for them in the inn.
LUKE 2:7

Reflection for leaders

'Children are the church of the future' is a phrase that is often trumpeted round church meetings, as people gather to discuss how to attract more children into church, or how to keep them quiet during the 'holy bits' of the service. Indeed, I have met many people who do not even hold that depressingly low view of the place of children in church, preferring instead to view Sunday school as a place where the young can be deposited in safe, if somewhat tedious, surroundings while the adults get on with the real business of worship. This, as we know, is very far from being the case. The church already belongs to children, as it does to all people, and their place within its life is every bit as valid as that of the most senior and long-serving churchwarden. The challenge of those working with young people is to enable both adult members of the congregation and the children themselves to recognise this.

It was no accident that Jesus broke into this fragile, damaged world as a baby, not as a fully grown adult. Just as his ministry provides us with a model for Christian thinking and living, so does his taking on the form of an infant give weight and dignity to that stage of human life. It was no accident either that the Messiah, the king, the Saviour was born in a manger—he had to be born somewhere, and the world would not offer him a place. We are told that there was no room for the Holy Family at the inn—but there is always room if someone is willing to share, to move some of their stuff, to go beyond their worries that there might not be enough and they don't want to miss out. Nobody made room, because this ordinary couple, rough-skinned through manual labour, did not look at all significant or important. The inhabitants of the inn took one look at them and suddenly the inn was so full that not even a small corner could be found for them. So that first Christmas, a food stall in a stable was provided for the arrival of a child.

The Church is here now, and it is our task, our calling, to

provide that manger, to be that place where the young, the 'unimportant', can find the nourishment they need to grow and flourish in this world.

Children's corners, areas, even dedicated rooms, are a wonderful asset to a church. They are a reminder that children have significance beyond their current size and understanding, that they are to be treated seriously as valued members of a church community. But it should never be forgotten that, just as the manger was not the extent of God's kingdom, so the children's corner is not a place where the children are confined but rather a base from which they can feel free to explore the whole of their church.

Bible story

The months passed quickly and soon the time came for Mary's baby to be born. It looked as though this would not happen in Nazareth, but in Bethlehem.

The Roman emperor, Caesar Augustus, wanted to tax his people. He ordered a census so that everyone had to go to the town of their ancestors to be counted. This meant that Joseph had to take Mary with him to Bethlehem, because he belonged to the family of King David.

Mary and Joseph made their way to the village of Bethlehem in Judea.

The roads were full of people travelling, all obeying the commands of their Roman ruler.

Bethlehem was bustling with people.

Men, women and children had all come to be registered there. By the time Mary and Joseph arrived, it was already difficult to find somewhere to stay.

Mary felt tired and weary; she was starting to feel the pains that meant her baby would soon be born.

Joseph went from house to house looking for a room because the inn was full. Eventually they found shelter where the animals were stabled.

That night, Mary gave birth to a baby boy, her first-born child. She wrapped him in strips of cloth and made a bed for him in a manger, because there was no room anywhere else.

'I wonder...'

I wonder how Mary and Joseph felt when no one wanted them...

I wonder what the people said when they were asked to make room for Mary and Joseph in the inn...

I wonder what Mary and Joseph felt when they realised their baby would be born in a stable...

I wonder what lying in a bed of hay feels like...

I wonder what Jesus could smell and hear in the stable...

Prayer activity

You will need:
- Shop-bought paper chains or strips of paper
- Glue sticks
- Crayons or pencils

Give each child a strip of paper and ask them either to write something they like about coming to church, or to draw a picture of themselves at church. If the group is not too big, ask those who wish to share what they have written or describe what they have drawn. If the children are too many, or too shy, invite conversation between them and the adult helpers, or ask them to tell the child sitting next to them about their part of the paper chain.

Explain that you are going to join all the strips of paper together to form a paper chain and help them to do this.

Once the paper chain is made, place it in the middle of your prayer circle and explain how, although individually the little strips of paper are quite small, they are very important because they all play a part in making up the long paper chain. Remind them that they are all important members of the church, and that just as Jesus started life on earth as a baby, then grew to be an adult who transformed the world, so each one of them will grow and contribute more and more to the life of the church. If possible, take the paper chain and hang it in the Sunday school room or children's corner.

Craft activities

Christmas tree

This tree is made out of the handprints of the children, reminding them that, although individually they may seem small, together they can create something significant and beautiful.

You will need:
- Red card
- A length of lining paper
- Green finger paint (the cleanest option is to

use purpose-designed paint pads, but paint in
a shallow dish will do, although it is definitely
messier!)
- Circular pieces of coloured card or paper, 8–10
cm in diameter
- Sequins, buttons, stickers and other decorations
- Glue

Cut a flower pot shape from the red card and stick it at one
end of the lining paper. This will be the Christmas tree tub.

Starting just above the tub, make handprints in a row
the width of the paper. The fingers need to be splayed and
pointing downwards to look like pine branches.

Make the tree as large as the paper/number of children
allows, gradually reducing the number of handprints per
row, so that you end at the top with a single, upside-down
hand print. It helps if you draw the rough outline of a triangle
before you start, to give you some idea of the shape that you
want to create.

Decorate the circular pieces of card with sequins, buttons
and other scraps, then glue them on to the Christmas tree.

If you wish, you can add a star at the top.

Matchbox nativity

You will need (per child):
- 1 matchbox: ask the congregation to start saving
these (in about April!) or buy white matchboxes
from a craft shop
- Blue paint
- 1 traditional wooden 'peg dolly' peg, which has

had the 'legs' sawn off just where it separates into two legs from the body of the peg
- Star, ideally of self-adhesive foam, the right size to fit on the top of the matchbox
- Tiny bit of hay or finely shredded paper
- A small scrap of white material (a bit of an old sheet is ideal)
- Washable PVA glue
- Black felt pen

First, paint the outside of the matchbox blue. Acrylic paint works best, but if you don't have any, mix some PVA glue in with the paint and it will stick better. Small children will need the matchboxes already painted.

While the matchbox is drying, make the baby.

Wrap the half peg in the scrap of white fabric and glue it in place.

Carefully draw on eyes and a mouth with the black pen.

When box and baby are dry, put a small amount of straw into the matchbox and then tuck the baby inside. Stick a star on the outside of the box.

Edible craft activities

Savoury Christmas tree

You will need (per child):
- 1 slice of bread
- About 10 mangetout peas (these can be eaten raw but are more digestible for small children if they have been plunged in boiling water for 2 minutes,

then rinsed in cold water); if mangetout are too
expensive or not appealing, you can use about 8
cm of cucumber
- A few slices of red pepper, plus one whole red
pepper
- 1 slice of processed cheese
- 2 slices of carrot
- Star-shaped cutter
- Christmas tree-shaped cutter (optional)
- Knife

Preparation

If you are working with very young children, you might want
to cut four of the mangetouts in half beforehand, and then
cut one end of each pea into a point. Cut another four into
two uneven lengths, about one third of the way along, and
then cut each piece into a point at one end. The final two can
be cut into quarters.

Cut the carrot slices into stars.

Cut one piece of red pepper into thin strips, working with
the shape of the pepper to give a curve to the strip.

Cut a flower-pot shape out of the remaining pepper.

Using the cutter or a knife, cut a Christmas tree shape out of
the bread.

Put the red pepper flower pot at the base of the bread
Christmas tree.

Starting at the bottom, layer the longest pieces of
mangetout with the pointed ends towards the pepper flower
pot, so that they look like pine branches. Then place the half
mangetouts on top, with the point of the pea pointing down,

and the main part overlapping the peas that are already there.

Next, add the layer of mangetouts that were one third long, and finally top with the quartered peas.

If you are using cucumber instead of mangetouts, slice the cucumber as thinly as you can, then cut the slices in half. Starting at the bottom, layer the cucumber on the tree, with the curved side facing towards the pot, and the half slices angled out towards the sides so that they look like pointed branches.

Put a carrot star on the top.

Decorate your tree with shapes cut out of the cheese slice and red pepper strips of 'tinsel'.

Sweet Christmas tree fairy cake

You will need (per child):
- 1 fairy cake
- 1 dsp of chocolate icing
- Small piece of red fondant icing
- 5 white mini marshmallows
- Yellow and green sugar sprinkles (optional: plus silver and/or gold sprinkles)

Spread the top of the fairy cake with chocolate icing. It doesn't have to be too smooth, as it will be mostly covered with marshmallows. If you wish, you can sprinkle gold or silver sprinkles on before adding the rest of the decorations.

With the red fondant icing, make a flower-pot shape and put it at the edge of the cake.

Cut the mini marshmallows in half.

Dip nine of the cut ends of the marshmallows in the green

sugar sprinkles, and one in the yellow, gold or silver.

Starting from the bottom, put four of the green-dipped marshmallows in a row, just above the red pot.

Follow this with a row of three, then a row of two.

Put the yellow, gold or silver-dipped marshmallow half on the top of the tree as the star.

*

Epiphany

Theme: looking beyond ourselves, the outside world

Place/object within the church building: roof

Suggested Bible passages

Old Testament: Isaiah 60:1–7

A multitude of camels shall cover you, the young camels of Midian and Ephah; all those from Sheba shall come. They shall bring gold and frankincense, and shall proclaim the praise of the Lord.

ISAIAH 60:6

New Testament: Matthew 2:11–12

On coming to the house, they saw the child with his mother Mary, and they bowed down and worshipped him. Then they opened their treasures and presented him with gifts of gold and of incense and of myrrh. And having been warned in a dream not to go back to Herod, they returned to their country by another route.

MATTHEW 2:11–12, NIV

Reflection for leaders

In one of the churches in which I worked, the roof of the nave was a work of art. Painted a wonderful sky-blue colour, it had gold stars of different sizes stencilled all over it. Merely to look up at it was to lose oneself in a panorama of blue and gold, encouraging thoughts to drift and float just as the stars themselves seemed to. On a Sunday morning, in the intervals between services, I would take my coffee up to the gallery in the tower and sit with my head among these stars, thinking about the service that had just finished, planning the next one, allowing my thoughts to roam freely and occasionally gaining moments of great insight from these mind journeys among the heavens.

Two thousand years ago, wise men, who had spent much time gazing upwards and outwards as they searched the heavens for signs, saw a new star and knew it indicated something unique and significant occurring in their world. They set out in faith to discover what this event might be, and the star led them to a family in an ordinary house in an ordinary village. What made them truly wise was the fact that they recognised within the apparent mundaneness of this family the future saviour of the world. The gifts they brought of gold, frankincense and myrrh recognised the roles Jesus would play in the future of humankind, as humble leader whose birth was of universal significance and whose death would free all people from death itself.

With the birth, death and resurrection of Jesus Christ, the war between good and evil was decisively and eternally won. A new world was ushered in, heaven on earth, God's kingdom come. Although the outcome is already decided, individual battles are still being fought, and that's where we come in. For counterbalancing the cosmic significance of the victory of Jesus Christ over the forces of evil is the fact that this victory took place in the context of the ordinary and the everyday, among the people of this earth. For this reason every action of our daily lives matters, every decision we make for right or wrong, every good word spoken, every helpful deed undertaken, all contribute towards that final victory. It is easy to underestimate the effects of what we do and what we say as we go about our everyday lives. But just as events in a small village changed the shape of the universe, so are our contributions to the battle of good versus evil played out on a cosmic scale. Every little act, every loving word, every prayer, counts.

It can be extremely rewarding occasionally simply to sit in the main body of a church and gaze up at the roof. Even if it is not painted with stars, it will probably be shaped like the upside-down hull of a ship, encouraging thoughts of strangeness, of things turned on their head. With pictures of ships come ideas of sea voyages, of exploring strange territories far away, of adventures and new lands. We can think new thoughts, dream dreams and look towards seeing these dreams realised. However, it is equally important to remember that our everyday actions, words and gestures also play a decisive part in fulfilling the promises made at the birth of that small baby so many years ago.

Bible story

Wise men living in the east had been studying the night skies when Jesus was born. They saw a strange new star and wondered what it could mean.

They set out on a journey, following the star, because they thought it heralded the birth of a new king, and they wanted to worship him.

When they reached Jerusalem, they stopped at King Herod's palace.

'Where is the child born to be king of the Jewish people?' they asked. 'We have come to pay our respects, to welcome and worship him.'

Herod was disturbed by their arrival. What king could there be apart from him? Quickly, Herod consulted the chief priests and teachers of the law. They told him what they knew from the ancient prophecies: the king would be born in Bethlehem.

Herod then talked to his eastern visitors and tried to find out exactly when they had first seen the star. This way he could know how old the baby might be. Then he sent them to Bethlehem.

'If you find the king,' he said craftily, 'let me know. I would like to be able to worship him as well.'

The wise men continued their journey until they reached Bethlehem, where the star seemed to stop over a house. They went inside and found Mary with her young child.

The wise men knew they had found the right place and worshipped Jesus, the new king. Then they gave him the gifts they had brought—gold, frankincense and myrrh.

They stopped for the night before beginning their return journey, but they did not go back the way they had come. In the night they had dreamed that it was not safe to return to King Herod.

'I wonder…'

I wonder what it would feel like to see a new star and know that it means the Saviour of the world has been born…

I wonder if the wise men were frightened when they decided to follow the star wherever it took them…

I wonder how the wise men felt when the star finally stopped moving and they realised they had come to the end of their journey…

I wonder what the wise men thought when they saw that the new king they had been looking for was only a child…

I wonder what present I would bring the new king…

Prayer activity

You will need (per child):
- A paper or cardboard star
- Crayons or a pencil

Begin by gathering the children into a group and get them to sit or ideally lie on the floor of the nave and look up at the ceiling. Ask them how it makes them feel to look up at something so far away. If the ceiling has any decorations, ask the children to describe the decorations and why they think the artist put them there. Remind them that the wise men had to journey for a long time from a long way away to find Jesus.

Once the children have sat up again, give each child a paper or cardboard star, and ask them to write their name on it. Once they have done this, take the children on a walk around the church building, making it as long as their concentration will allow. Depending on the type of church, you might want to use some incense to head up your procession, reminding the children that one of the gifts of the wise men was frankincense, which was used to help people pray. End your procession either at the crib, if your church has one, or at the altar. Ask the children to lay their stars as gifts for the baby, born to be the Saviour of the world.

Craft activities

Gift box

You will need:
- Selection of empty boxes and cartons with lids (use margarine tubs, shoe boxes or chocolate boxes, or buy blank cardboard boxes from craft shops)
- Paint (for blank boxes, poster paint will do; other boxes may require acrylic paint to cover up logos or text)
- Collage materials, like sequins, feathers, buttons, ribbon, foam letters

Preparation

If the children are young or time is short, you can paint the boxes beforehand in a selection of colours.

Make treasure boxes by decorating the boxes as lavishly as possible. If you wish, you can put some of the star biscuits (see p. 61) inside and give them as an Epiphany gift.

Lolly stick star

This is a very simple activity, yet produces good results for every age group.

You will need:
- 8 craft sticks per star (coloured craft sticks are fun, but are not absolutely necessary as lots of decoration will cover up the stick anyway)
- Strong glue (a glue gun is best for this)
- Thread or wool
- Sequins, glitter, beads or other decorations
- Washable PVA glue

Preparation

Glue eight craft sticks into the shape of a star, then leave to dry.

If you are working with very young children, you might want to attach a loop of thread to one of the sticks so that the star can be hung up. This has the advantage of enabling the finished stars to be hung up to dry, giving them less chance of sticking to the newspaper, tablecloth or table!

Decorate the stars with whatever you have. It can be very useful for using up leftover scraps of tinsel or ends of glitter glue.

Edible craft activities

It is not easy to do either of these crafts without at least one star-shaped biscuit cutter. There will be plenty available in the Christmas season, and it is a good idea to buy more than one, preferably of different sizes.

Savoury starry night tortilla

You will need (per child):
- 1 tortilla
- Edible raw vegetables, such as red, green and yellow peppers, cucumber, celery, radishes
- Mayonnaise or salad cream
- Knife for cutting vegetables
- Star-shaped cutters

Cut out star shapes from the vegetables and arrange on the tortilla, using mayonnaise or salad cream to 'stick' them on.

Young children may need the vegetables presliced so that all they need to do is cut star shapes from them.

This craft can be adapted using slices of fruit on teacakes or syrup pancakes if the sweet craft below contains too much sugar for personal taste!

Sweet star biscuits

You will need (per child):
- 2 or 3 star-shaped biscuits
- Fondant icing, ideally in different colours, or in yellow or white
- Rolling pin
- Baking paper
- Star-shaped cutter, ideally in a smaller size than that used to make the biscuits
- Some sugar stars (found among the cake decorations in most supermarkets)
- Some sieved jam
- A very clean, ideally unused paintbrush

Place a small amount of fondant icing between two sheets of baking paper and roll out to the required size. (If you are using banqueting roll to cover your tables, the baking paper is not necessary as the icing does not stick to it.)

Cut out star shapes with the cutter.

Stick the fondant stars on to the biscuits using the sieved jam.

Paste more jam on top of the icing and scatter it with sugar stars.

*

Baptism of Christ

Theme: baptism

Place/object within the church building: font

Suggested Bible passages

Old Testament: Genesis 1:1–5

In the beginning when God created the heavens and the earth, the earth was a formless void and darkness covered the face of the deep, while a wind from God swept over the face of the waters.

GENESIS 1:1–2

New Testament: Mark 1:4–11

And just as he was coming out of the water, he saw the heavens torn apart and the Spirit descending like a dove on him. And a voice came from heaven, 'You are my Son, the Beloved; with you I am well pleased.'

MARK 1:10–11

Reflection for leaders

The baptism of Christ falls after Epiphany, before Candlemas, when our thoughts turn finally towards Lent and Good Friday. For most of us, the Christmas season ended a while back. Everyone is back at work, children are at school, and even the supermarkets have mostly stopped trying to sell us cut-price Christmas puddings. The great drama is over, and it is difficult not to gaze about us and ask, now what? Mary and Joseph have had their son; the visitors have left; the excitement is over. We are, after all, still waiting, here on the other side of Christmas, for the work to begin—and here at this festival, it does. A young man stands on the edge of a riverbank, dripping wet. A voice speaks to him, God's voice. In Mark's version of the story, only Jesus can hear the voice; it is personal, intimate, meant for him alone. It doesn't give Jesus a list of instructions as to how to begin his ministry, or a series of warnings of the pitfalls to avoid, or even a set of targets that he must achieve. Instead, the creator of the universe whispers into the ear of his Son, 'You are my beloved. With you I am well pleased.'

The whole story of Jesus' ministry begins with words of affirmation. Before Jesus had preached a single word or healed a single person, God speaks to him in words of love, demonstrating the foundation stone of grace that will sustain Christ and, if we allow it, sustain us as well. Because at our baptism, these words are spoken to us as well. Laying aside any talk of sin or forgiveness, baptism fundamentally celebrates the love that God has for us, the fact that we are his children, his sons, his daughters, his beloved ones. Baptism affirms the worth of each and every person in the eyes of God. It reminds us that God's love always remains unconditional, that we can depend upon it, whatever we do. Wonderful words, reminding us that each time we fall short of the life God wants for us in the way we speak or act, there is no condemnation waiting at the moment of our repentance, only loving forgiveness and a renewal of the promise of hope made at Christ's birth.

How should we respond to this profound affirmation that we have received as children of God? Well, by seeking to affirm others. We should create an atmosphere of encouragement, praise, acceptance and love, not in an empty or hypocritical way, not by praising indiscriminately or needlessly, but in recognition of the uniqueness of each of God's creations and gratefulness for sharing time with them. We are all his beloved, and he is well pleased with us all.

Bible story

Jesus came to the River Jordan one day. He was now a man of about 30 and had been a carpenter for many years.

Jesus stepped forward as John was calling people to be baptised.

John knew straight away who he was. He also knew he was not worthy to baptise Jesus!

But Jesus persuaded him. He told John it was what God wanted. As Jesus came out of the water, God's Spirit came down from heaven like a dove and rested on Jesus. A voice from heaven said: 'This is my Son. I love you very much. I am pleased with you.'

'I wonder...'

I wonder what John thought when Jesus wanted to be baptised by him...

I wonder what it felt like in the river Jordan...

I wonder what I would think if I saw a dove appear from heaven...

I wonder how Jesus felt when God told him he was pleased with him...

I wonder what Jesus did afterwards...

Prayer activity

You will need:
- Font or a large shallow bowl
- Large candle
- Jug of water
- Simple paper flower shapes (petal shapes around a circular centre are best)
- Water-soluble felt pens

If you have a font in your church, take the children to stand in a circle around the font. It may be too big for them to see comfortably over the top; that is all right, as it brings in a sense of mystery. If you have no font, place a large, shallow bowl in the middle of your prayer circle. Set a large candle (the larger the better) next to the font; if you have a Paschal candle, use that.

Explain that this is where people of all ages are welcomed into the family of God. Tell the children that the water is used as a sign that just as when we play with paint or mud or get our hands dirty and need to wash them to make them clean, so when we say or do things that are not kind, the fact that we have been washed in the water of baptism means that when we say sorry we are made clean inside. Baptism means we have to be washed clean inside only once, unlike our hands, which need washing all the time.

Ask the children to think of things that they might do or say that are not kind, either to themselves or to other people. You can suggest things like saying something horrid or not helping other people. Try to keep it general.

Give each child a paper flower and ask them to write or draw one of these things in the centre of the flower. They can choose the same thing as someone else or something different.

Once the flowers have been written on, fold the petals into the centre on top of each other.

Pour some of the water into the font.

Gently float the petals on top of the water. Watch as the petals gradually unfold and the water gradually covers the centre of the petals and washes the writing or drawing away. This can take some time and, depending on the age of the group, you might either want to play some reflective music while this happens, or hurry along the washing away process by deliberately sinking the flowers.

Explain to the children that when we say sorry to God for the things we have done, these things are washed away and forgiven.

Light the candle as a sign of God's love for every person in the group and as a promise that God will always be with them.

Craft activities

Bubbles

This is a messy activity but a lot of fun.

You will need:
- Coloured poster paint
- Water
- Large shallow dish
- Washing-up liquid
- Drinking straws
- Thick blue paper or thin card
- White paper
- Yellow and black crayons
- Scissors
- Glue sticks

This craft has two stages. For the first, mix up some coloured paint thinned with a little water and pour it into the shallow dish. Then mix in some washing-up liquid. You will need to experiment beforehand to make sure you have got the proportions of paint to washing-up liquid correct, as this will depend on the size of the dish you are using.

With older children, this experimentation can be part of the activity; if your group is too young to be patient, it is best to work this out beforehand.

Using the drinking straws, blow into the paint solution until it is a mass of bubbles.

If you are working with young children, make sure that they have grasped the principle of blowing through a straw rather than sucking. Test them first by asking them to blow on your hands with the straw.

When a mass of bubbles has risen well above the level of the dish, gently place a sheet of blue paper or card on top of the bubbles, then quickly take it off again. It may take some time to get the technique quite right, so it is best to have an ample supply of paper.

Hang the bubble picture up to dry.

While the pictures are drying, using the white paper, ask the children to draw round their hands with their thumb outstretched but their fingers all closed together.

Cut out the dove shape. Make the thumb into a bird's head by drawing a yellow beak right on the end and adding an eye.

Glue the dove on to the middle of the bubble picture.

Paper dove

You will need:
- Thin white card
- White tissue paper, cut into rectangles
- Wobbly eyes or black crayon
- Sequins, buttons and other decorations
- Cardboard template of a dove's body (either invent a general bird shape or find a pattern from the internet)
- Scissors
- Glue sticks
- Wool (optional)

Draw round the dove template on to the white card and cut it out.

Cut a slit about 1.5 cm long in the middle of the dove's body where the wings will go. An adult might need to help with this to prevent the slit being too long or tearing.

Decorate the dove's body with sequins, ribbons, buttons and so on.

Fold the tissue paper into a concertina shape.

Gently push the tissue paper through the slit in the dove's body. This again can be tricky and an adult's help might be welcome.

Fan out the tissue paper to look like wings.

If you wish, you can make a hole in the top of the dove's body and thread a loop of wool to enable the dove to be hung up.

Edible craft activities

Savoury font

You will need (per child):
- 1 crusty bread roll (the best are those with flat bottoms but rounded tops and quite a firm crust)
- 1 dsp of houmous
- Margarine for spreading
- Blue food colouring
- Knife and spoon

First of all, cut the top off the bread roll and set it to one side.

Cut the edges off the side of the bread to make an octagon; first cut the roll into a square shape, then cut the edges off each corner. Try to make the sides as equal as possible. An adult may need to help with this.

Dig out the soft centre of the bread roll until a basin shape is achieved. Too much enthusiasm will lead to an erosion of the sides, so take care with this.

Mix the houmous with the blue food colouring until a watery shade is achieved.

Gently spoon the houmous into the bread font.

Flatten the top of the bread roll piece that was sliced off at the beginning.

Spread some margarine on the flat top and use it to 'glue' the font on to the bread roll piece so that it looks like the foot of the font.

Sweet dove

You will need (per child):
- 1 fairy cake
- Vanilla buttercream icing
- White fondant icing
- Black and yellow writing icing
- Red sprinkles (optional)

Cover the top of the fairy cake with buttercream icing and then dip it in red sprinkles, if you have these.

With the white fondant icing, make a dove. It is easiest to make each component separately (wings, body and so on).

Use the yellow writing icing to make a beak.

Place the dove on top of the fairy cake.

*

Candlemas

Suggested Bible passages

Old Testament: Malachi 3:1–4

See, I am sending my messenger to prepare the way before me, and the Lord whom you seek will suddenly come to his temple.

MALACHI 3:1A

New Testament: Luke 2:22–40

For my eyes have seen your salvation, which you have prepared in the presence of all peoples.

LUKE 2:30–31

Reflection for leaders

One of the triumphs of Christmas is that of the overthrow of expectations, of the world's way of doing things. The Jewish nation were looking for a king, a powerful leader, a warrior. They were given a baby born in a stable. At Candlemas we revisit this theme, but with an additional promise: that however dark things appear to become in our lives, the light of Christ is always shining, even if sometimes we cannot see it.

Candlemas celebrates the presentation of Christ in the temple, a tradition in those times. The story emphasises the ordinariness of the occasion, and even the fact that the family only bring doves as a sacrifice, because they could not afford lambs. Yet Simeon recognises the Christ. In this tiny baby lie the hopes of the world, hopes that will be fulfilled through his life and death. The church takes up the words of Simeon when he calls the child a light to lighten the Gentiles and makes of this occasion a feast of candles, a time when traditionally the year's supply of candles for the church was blessed. Today, this aspect of the feast is less important, but for many centuries, the church could be lit only by candlelight; services in the depth of winter would be characterised by the deep shadows surrounding the congregation, illuminated only by small pools of brightness at the lectern and the altar. How powerful, then, would the symbol of the light shining in the darkness be! The candlelight is a tangible reminder of that greater light which for and beyond all time radiates from the figure of Jesus. In the early Christian era, the Candlemas procession replaced a riotous pagan carnival in which magical powers were invoked to repel evil spirits from the city. In Candlemas, the wild cry for deliverance is met with the constant, unfailing light of Christ.

Candlemas has a bitter-sweet nature to it. It is a feast day, and the revelation of the child Jesus in the temple calls for rejoicing. But the prophetic words of Simeon speak of the falling and rising of many. He addresses Jesus' mother Mary and tells her of a sword that will pierce her heart, and in so doing leads us to turn our face towards Good Friday. Candlemas is a pivotal point in the Christian year—one last look at Christmas and then we turn towards the cross.

The feast reminds us that at the heart of Christianity, hope and the cross reside together. This very duality means that the difficult times of our lives cannot overwhelm them, because even when the world seems very dark indeed, the light of Christ remains shining. Remember that, in complete darkness, it only takes one small candle to bring in the light.

Candles remind us of the hope that lies in Christ, of the love that will bridge the gap between where we are and where we want to be, of the companion who walks beside us on our journey. The light of candles is small and easily put out, but this merely emphasises the immensity of the one whose light can never be extinguished.

Bible story

When Jesus was just over a month old, Mary and Joseph prepared to take him to the temple in Jerusalem. They went to thank God for his safe birth and offer a sacrifice of two pigeons.

As they went into the temple courts, they met there a man called Simeon. Simeon had been waiting for the day when God would send his Messiah—the chosen one who would save his people. He believed that God had promised him that he would see this Saviour before he died.

When Simeon saw Mary and Joseph and the baby boy in their arms, he knew that the special day had arrived. He took Jesus from them and praised God.

'Lord, you can let me now die in peace, because I have

seen with my own eyes the Saviour you have promised to your people. This child will reveal your truth to all people on earth and be everything the Jewish nation have been waiting for.'

Mary and Joseph listened in some surprise to his words, but before they had taken it all in, an elderly woman approached them. Anna was a prophetess who had lived in the temple, praying and worshipping God for most of her long life. She also knew that Jesus was God's chosen one. And she thanked God for him.

Mary and Joseph made their offering. They wondered at all they had learned that day about their baby son.

'I wonder…'

I wonder what Mary and Joseph expected to happen when they went to the temple…

I wonder how they felt when two strangers came up to them and said wonderful things about Jesus…

I wonder what Mary thought when Simeon told her that difficult times were coming…

I wonder which parts of this story remind me of Christmas…

I wonder which parts of this story make me think of Good Friday and Easter…

Prayer activity

As with any activity involving candles, take great care to keep the children away from the flames. Before the prayer activity begins, remind them that candles and matches are dangerous and only adults should light candles. If working with more than one candle, make sure you have enough adult helpers, and know where the fire safety equipment is.

Candles have tremendous visual power, and often the simple action of lighting a candle and placing it in the centre of a prayer circle can have a quietening effect. All that is required from the leader is encouragement to focus on the flame and become aware of the stillness. However, sometimes a more interactive prayer activity can be helpful.

For this activity you will need several candles. Ideally, one should be bigger and taller than the others, and there should be three identical candles and a smaller, thinner one. In addition, you could have a candle to give to each child at the end but that is optional. Place them together in the centre of the prayer circle. Remind the children that Simeon called Jesus a light. Light the tallest, biggest candle and ask them what they think that might mean. Encourage reflections on Jesus' love for other people, making them feel happier and brighter. Help the children to think about the symbol of darkness for feeling sad or frightened, and how Jesus might help those feelings to be less acute.

Lead the children from thinking about the light of Christ to thinking about how other people can show that light; how the way people live their lives can be a light for others, in that they help the darkness to disappear, and how different these ways may be. Indicate the tall candle and ask them to think of ways in which teachers and leaders can bring light. Introduce a moment of silence while you thank God for all that they do.

A group of three identical candles can indicate families, people who love you. Help the children to think of some of the ways in which these people make them feel better if they are sad, or help them to celebrate when things are going well. Finally, light the last candle. This is for each individual. Tell the children that although the candle is smaller than the others, the flame is the same size—it doesn't matter how big or powerful you seem to be, you can still have the same effect on others. Ask the children to think of ways in which they might bring light to others in the way they talk and act. In a moment of silence, encourage them to reflect on these ways and to ask God to help them. If you have enough candles and adult helpers, each child can be given a candle to hold, lit from the 'Jesus' candle, reminding the children that the love and the hope that we bring to others is first given to us from Christ.

Craft activities

Mosaic candle

This is a variation on the usual toilet roll candle craft. It takes slightly longer, and older children will also find it enjoyable.

You will need (per child):
- 1 toilet roll
- 1 sheet of white paper
- Small squares of coloured paper (tissue paper is a bit fragile when glueing, and card is too stiff; cut the squares really quite small, no bigger than 1 cm, or they will not glue properly to the curve of the candle)
- Green paper or card
- 1 foam heart, or one large orange foam heart and two smaller yellow hearts
- Cotton wool ball

Cut the sheet of white paper to the size of the toilet roll and stick it on. You might want to do this prior to the activity, as the mosaic pieces become quite difficult to stick on if too much glue is used.

Cut a circle out of the green card and stick the toilet roll upright on to it, so that the green circle forms a stand.

With the coloured squares of paper, create a mosaic pattern on the toilet roll candle. This can be as simple or complex as the age of the child dictates.

When the mosaic is finished, fluff out the cotton wool ball and stick it just inside the top of the candle.

Invert the foam heart(s) and glue it/them to the top of the cotton wool to act as the flame.

Candlestick

You will need:
- Air-dry clay (ideally coloured, because it looks nicer when it is dry; mail order craft suppliers now sell some big 2 kg tubs in white or terracotta, which look better than the standard grey, although they are a bit more expensive)
- Supply of cheap household candles (to be found in DIY shops or larger supermarkets)
- Buttons and other small objects for decoration (if you use upholstery pins, nails or washers, great care should be taken with these around young children as they present a choking hazard)
- Knives, clay shaping tools and other objects for making patterns

Take a piece of air-dry clay and form it into a ball.

Push the candle firmly into the centre of the ball. This will also have the effect of flattening the bottom of the clay so that it provides a stable base.

Make sure the candle is fast within the candlestick, shaping the clay if necessary.

Decorate the candlestick with the objects provided, making patterns with the tools and other objects.

Encourage the children to search round the church looking for objects to push into the clay or with which to make patterns. Make sure they ask your permission before using any object in this way!

Allow the candlestick to dry with the candle still in it, as this ensures stability.

Edible craft activities

Savoury candle

You will need (per child):
- 1 pitta bread
- Mayonnaise or margarine for spreading
- All or some of the following: slice of ham, slice of processed cheese, slice each of red and green pepper, stick of celery
- Knife for cutting

Preparation

For young children, cut out several identical 'flame' shapes from the cheese. You might also need to cut the other food into candle shapes, making sure they differ in length and width.

Cut one of the long ends of the pitta bread so that it is flat at the bottom. This is not absolutely necessary but makes a nice base and has the effect of creating a dome shape above the candle 'flames'.

From the ham and vegetables, cut a number of candle shapes. Make sure they are different sizes and widths.

Place them along the straight edge of the pitta, 'glueing' them in place with mayonnaise or margarine.

Cut several 'flame' shapes from the cheese slice. Try to make them identical—the message is that although human beings, like candles, are all different, the light of Christ within them is the same.

Place the 'flame' shapes on top of the candles.

Sweet candle

You will need (per child):
- 1 digestive biscuit
- 1 quantity of buttercream icing, plain or coloured
- 1 chocolate mini roll
- Rice paper
- Sugar letters or other decorations (optional)

Cover the digestive biscuit with the buttercream icing.

Stick the mini roll on to the biscuit.

Place a small amount of buttercream on top of the mini roll.

Cut a flame shape from the rice paper and stick it into the

buttercream.
Decorate the candle and the base.

*

Ash Wednesday/Lent

Theme: sharing what we have; making sacrifices

Place/object within the church building: kitchen or welcome area

Suggested Bible passages

Old Testament: Isaiah 58:6–12

Is not this the fast that I choose: to loose the bonds of injustice, to undo the thongs of the yoke, to let the oppressed go free, and to break every yoke?
ISAIAH 58:6

New Testament: Matthew 6:1–6

When you give alms, do not let your left hand know what your right hand is doing, so that your alms may be done in secret; and your Father who sees in secret will reward you.
MATTHEW 6:3–4

Reflection for leaders

Some years ago, when my children were very little, we went on a family holiday to a Christian retreat centre. It was a beautiful place, right by the sea, and the children loved having the freedom of the big old house and huge garden to play in. By chance, there were a lot of very young children and babies on that particular holiday week, and every mealtime the dining hall would run out of teaspoons. This should not really have mattered, except that it made feeding my youngest child, who was only eight months old at the time, a little problematic. The domestic team were very helpful but also rather perplexed: as soon as they realised that there was a shortage of teaspoons, they had gone out and bought some more, and could not understand why there were still not enough. Nor could I, until I sat on a table with a mother who smugly brandished the three teaspoons she had picked up as soon as she came in. Why three? Who knows! She just knew there was a shortage and wanted there to be enough for her child. So I sat there wedging a dessertspoon into Ellie's baby mouth while she held on to her two spare spoons...

Every year, many people decide to 'give something up' for Lent, whether it is chocolate or alcohol, shopping or watching too much television. It seems to have become more popular than ever, perhaps because a mood of self-denial fits in well with the current desire for self-improvement. This is to miss the point completely, for Lent is not about retreating into the desert so that a newer, better, faster self can emerge. It is about focusing on important issues by letting go of the unimportant ones. It is about focusing on God and, through God, on those with whom we share our lives.

Living Lent well is not about a personal, private path to paradise. It is about making the deliberate choice to put God and other people first, to limiting ourselves to what is 'enough' in recognition of the needs of others. The message of Lent is a challenge to each one of us to examine our lives, to look at all that we do, how we treat our families, and how we act at work, and ask ourselves if we are taking the easy way, or if there is something we can do to be a more loving and caring person.

The place in the church that has been chosen to symbolise Lent is the kitchen. One of the reasons for this is that it is in the area of food and drink that most people are tempted to take more than their fair share, not necessarily through eating too much, but through eating unwisely, without due thought as to the origin of that food and the effect its production might be having on the wider world. The other reason is because it is in the kitchen that most opportunities for hospitality begin, in the preparation of food and drink for others, in the offering of ourselves for cleaning and serving duties, in sharing with other people the gifts that have been given to us.

Lent should be a time for personal reflection and private prayer, but it is also a time for sharing what we have with others, so that they too might live well.

Bible story

After his baptism, Jesus was led by God's Spirit into the desert. He went without food for 40 days and at the end of this time Jesus was weak and very hungry.

God's enemy, the devil, tried to test Jesus.

'You need food,' he said. 'If you are God's Son, you can make this stone turn into bread.'

'Life is more than just food,' replied Jesus, quoting God's law.

Then the devil led Jesus to a very high place and showed

him all the kingdoms of the world.

'Look at all this!' whispered the devil. 'I will give it to you, if you bow down and worship me.'

'God has said that we must worship him alone,' replied Jesus.

Then the devil took Jesus to Jerusalem. They stood on the highest part of the temple.

'God has promised to send his angels to protect you,' continued the devil. 'Throw yourself off the temple, so we can see his power!'

'God's law says that we must not put him to the test,' Jesus replied.

The devil had tried to tempt Jesus to break God's laws and do something wrong, but Jesus would not give in. The devil left, and Jesus was alone.

'I wonder...'

I wonder what it would be like not to see anyone for 40 days and nights...

I wonder what Jesus prayed about when he was in the desert...

I wonder how hungry Jesus felt after he had been in the desert...

I wonder what it would be like to be offered such a lot of things...

I wonder what was the first thing Jesus did after he came out...

Prayer activity

The focus of prayer for children in Lent does not always have to be on what each child might 'give up'. This has dangers, particularly for young children, in that it becomes an effort of will and a personal triumph, rather than an acceptance of dependence on God and a time for personal humility. Failure to maintain the particular sacrifice might obscure its original purpose in the same way as if the child were to succeed. Another way could be to turn the focus outward to how the children can improve the lives of those around them by what they do and say, or how they can share the gifts they have with others. One way of doing this is a 'good deed tree'.

Find a large, attractive branch and place it in a pot or vase. The branch needs to have lots of smaller branches, and be robustly fixed in the pot. It needs to be sturdy enough to last the entire 40 days of Lent, so choose it carefully. It does not have to be alive—some of the decorative branches left from Christmas can be just right for this purpose.

Using stiff paper or thin card, cut out enough leaves for each child in your group to have six. Punch holes in one end of these leaves and thread a loop of wool so that they can be hung or tied on to the branch.

Place the good deed tree in the centre of the prayer circle and give each child six leaves. Explain that these will be 'good deed leaves' and that they are to be hung on the tree when a good deed is done by the child. Talk to the children about what such a 'good deed' might be: depending on the age of the children, this might be helping with domestic chores, going to bed without making a fuss, looking after other children, or saying and doing something kind and thoughtful. The leaves can then be used in a number of ways, depending on the nature and age of your group. Each child can take home their blank leaves, which can be filled in by themselves or an adult when a good deed is done. The leaves can then be brought back to the church on a weekly basis, or at the end of Lent, and hung on the tree. An alternative is for the children to decide among themselves on one good deed per week that every child will try to carry out. The children can write or draw this on the leaves and then place them in a bowl at the base of the tree. At each subsequent meeting during Lent, leaves can be hung on the tree as the children share what they did and look forward to the next week. It is important not to make this too inquisitorial, and to allow each child to hang a leaf on the tree or not as they choose. The session can end with some time to think about the people they are going to help and to thank God for the opportunity of helping.

Craft activities

Desert picture

You will need:
- 2 large pieces of lining paper of equal size
- Blue paint and brushes
- Sand
- Washable PVA glue and brushes
- Stones and small pieces of dried twigs
- Yellow card
- Scissors

This will be a large collage of a desert scene. If you can make the gathering of sticks and stones part of the art activity, so much the better; just try not to get the stones too big or they will not glue properly to the paper.

Cover the first piece of paper with blue paint and allow to dry (you can do this yourself prior to the activity if you are short of time).

Cut the second piece of paper roughly in half horizontally, making the cut jagged and uneven to look like the edge of a desert landscape. This will be the sand section.

If you have a large group of children, it might be easier to divide the lining paper into smaller sections, then fasten it together at the end of the activity. Give each child a section of paper to paste with glue and then sprinkle sand on to it as a background, and encourage them to stick on stones and twigs as part of a group. This avoids the danger of one child being in sole charge of the glue.

When the sand scene is dry, stick it to the blue sky paper. This will have the advantage of making the scene more robust than if you had simply painted the sky on to the same piece of paper.

With the yellow card, make a large, bright sun and stick it up in the top corner.

Margarine money box

As part of the theme of sharing, this money box can be made on the understanding that the money collected in it goes to a charity or to the church at the end of Lent.

You will need (per child):
- 1 margarine or butter tub with a lid
- Scissors
- Acrylic paint
- Masking tape
- Washable PVA glue
- Old magazines
- Sequins and other decorations
- Permanent marker pen

Cut a gap in the lid for the money to go in. This is quite tricky and may require adult help, depending on the age of the children.

Paint the margarine tub and lid with acrylic paint. You can use poster paint mixed with PVA glue, but the coverage is not so good. As it is, you may need to use two coats. If the activity takes place over two sessions, you can use one for the painting; if not, it is best to paint these beforehand and allow them to dry.

If you are painting the boxes beforehand, you may want to tape the lid to the box with masking tape or duct tape before painting over it. This avoids the constant opening of the box to count the money. On the other hand, you may wish keeping count to be part of the activity.

Ask the children to cut out of the magazines pictures of people they might like to help with the money they save. Depending on the age of the children and the type of magazine, this might be simply pictures of any people. However, if you can get hold of relevant charity magazines or church newspapers, you have the opportunity to make these pictures much more relevant.

After the children have stuck these pictures on the side of

the boxes, they can fill in any gaps with other decorations.

Write the child's name and what the money box is in aid of on top of the box. The box can be brought to church on Easter Day and included in the offertory.

Edible craft activities

Savoury Lenten fish

You will need (per child):
- 2 tbsps of white rice, cooked and left to cool
- Small handful of tortilla chips (or crisps)
- 1 stick of celery
- 1 tomato
- 1 yellow pepper
- 2 Babybel® cheese or similar
- Knife for cutting

Spread the white rice out on a plate to form a square or rectangle.

Crush the tortilla chips into small pieces and spread carefully at the bottom edge of the rice. This will form the gravel sea bed.

Make the fish using stripes of pepper and cheese. Cut the head of the fish out of a semicircle of yellow pepper or use a quarter of tomato. Cut a slice of cheese and put it up against the head, then cut another slice from the pepper and tomato and finish with a slice of cheese. Cut a tail from the pepper or a quarter piece of tomato sliced in half.

Slice the celery into thin strips, making sure that the strips stay attached together at one end. This will make some weed.

Sweet Lenten fish

You will need (per child):
- Kiwi fruit
- 1 slice of mandarin orange or clementine
- 1 strawberry
- 1 grape
- Blue jelly (optional) (if you can't find blue jelly, use lemon jelly with a few drops of blue food colouring added)

If you are using jelly, mash this up and place it in a bowl to look like the sea.

Peel the kiwi fruit and slice it in half vertically. Put it on the jelly or on a plate.

Cut the orange slice in half and use as fins. Cut the grape in half and place it as the tail.

Cut a slice of strawberry vertically, using the middle of the strawberry. Place the 'pointed' end against the head of the fish as a mouth.

Put some strawberry where the fish eye should be. You might want to dig a bit out of the kiwi to sit the strawberry in so that it does not roll about too much.

*

Mothering Sunday

Theme: saying thank you; the Mother Church

Place/object within the church building: flowers

Suggested Bible passages

Old Testament: 1 Samuel 1:1–28

Therefore I have lent him to the Lord; as long as he lives he is given to the Lord.

1 SAMUEL 1:28

New Testament: John 19:25b–27

When Jesus saw his mother and the disciple whom he loved standing beside her, he said to his mother, 'Woman, here is your son.' Then he said to the disciple, 'Here is your mother.'

JOHN 19:26–27A

Reflection for leaders

Flowers and Mothering Sunday have always been closely linked, dating back to the 1600s in England, when young people who worked away from home were traditionally given the day off to visit their parents. Returning home, often after a significant length of time and from quite a distance, these young men and women would bring their mothers gifts of flowers. As time passed, it became traditional for all children to give their mothers bunches of flowers on Mothering Sunday, as a token of thanks for their care and love over the past year. Those whose mothers had died would place the flowers on the grave and say prayers for their souls.

The honouring of parents is one of the ten commandments. From the Middle Ages in England, people would also take the opportunity given by the break in fasting offered on the fourth Sunday in Lent to bring flowers and offerings to their local church, their 'mother church', a source of life and spiritual power.

There is more. Mothering Sunday celebrates love. It celebrates the love of the church for its people and of a mother for her children. It celebrates the endless, self-sacrificing, constantly giving love that enables the church to accept all people under its wings, and the mother to forgive her children again and again for the hurts they cause her. Mothering Sunday reminds us of the difficulties of living together, as family, as community, as congregation, and of the importance of small gestures of recognition and thankfulness that smoothe communal living and make it harmonious. Mother Teresa, not a mother at all, summed up motherhood and life in community, lived with other people, with the words:

'We can do no great things, only small things with great love.'

Mothering Sunday is a celebration of small things, done with great love, even if it is only the offering of a posy of flowers to members of our congregation.

Bible story

John, one of Jesus' disciples, was standing near the foot of the cross. A group of women, including Jesus' own mother, was also there.

'Dear woman,' Jesus said to Mary, 'treat this man as your son. John,' he then said to his friend, 'treat this woman as if she were your mother.'

'I wonder...'

I wonder what Jesus was thinking about his mother...
I wonder how Mary felt when she saw her son on the cross, in such pain...
I wonder what John felt when he heard what Jesus said...
I wonder what John said to Mary...
I wonder what John and Mary did next...

Prayer activity

You will need:
- Brightly coloured card, in at least two colours
- 2 large circles of orange or yellow card
- Large piece of stiff paper
- Glue, scissors, felt pens
- Bunch or pot of flowers

If the children are young, cut out enough petals from the coloured card for every child to have two each before the prayer activity. The large circles of card will make the centre of the flower, with the petals arranged around the outside.

If the children are old enough, provide them with a couple of cardboard templates that they can take in turns to use to cut out petals from card, encouraging the idea of giving and sharing in a group.

When all the petals are ready, place the bunch or pot of flowers in the centre of the circle. Tell the children that flowers have traditionally been associated with Mothering Sunday as a way of saying thank you to the people who look after them and love them. Be sensitive to the needs of those who have a primary carer who is not their mother, including all sorts of carers and different ways of being in families and showing love to each other.

If the group is able to do this, spend some time in quiet, just looking at the flowers and feeling thankful.

Encourage the children to write or draw one way in which their mother or primary carer looks after them or shows love for them. Take it in turns to stick the petals round one of the flower centres.

When the flower is made, remind the children that the church is a place where people are cared for, and discuss some ways in which a church might care for people and show love for each other and the wider world. Ask the children how they feel when they are in church, and to list the people who look after them there.

Allow the children time to write or draw some of these things on their second petal, which can then be stuck around the second flower centre.

Glue the two flowers side by side on the large sheet of paper. If there is time, give the children space to look at the flowers and discuss other people's thoughts and drawings.

Craft activities

Flower pot

You will need (per child):
- 1 small terracotta flower pot
- Bulb compost
- Old dessertspoon
- 2 or 3 small bulbs (if you buy these from a garden centre you can get advice as to which are best to buy)
- Acrylic paint
- Self-adhesive foam letters and other decorations
- Dry cloth
- Large shallow container (optional)

These are very simple to make: if you have two sessions or one quite long session, paint the flower pots and then let them dry. If you don't have much time, you will need to paint them beforehand.

If you have a reasonable number of children, it is fun to tip the compost into a large shallow container—those plastic drawers that go under beds are perfect. Then provide each child with a pot and a spoon, and they can dig up the compost for as long as they like before filling the flower pot.

Fill the pot about two-thirds full before gently planting the bulbs, then topping it up with compost.

Once the bulbs are planted, wipe the outside of the pots with a dry cloth to dislodge any excess compost, then take the pot to a different activity area to decorate.

Any decorations are suitable, but self-adhesive foam letters can be used to spell the name of the recipient.

Over time, these letters can occasionally come unstuck, especially if the pot is enthusiastically watered. Stick them back with washable PVA glue.

Paper flower

You will need (per child):
- Paper in two or three different colours
- 1 button with holes large enough for a pipe cleaner to fit through
- 1 green pipe cleaner
- 1 flower template
- Scissors

Using the template, cut out several flowers from the coloured paper. You can use tissue paper, but this will be a bit flimsy for younger children. If the paper is too stiff, the pipe cleaner won't push through it, so experiment a little beforehand.

Place the paper flowers on top of each other, and put the button on top.

Push a pipe cleaner through one button hole and the paper flowers, pushing four-fifths of the pipe cleaner through to the underside of the flower.

Push the shorter end through the other button hole and paper flowers, then turn the flower upside down.

Twist the long and the short ends of pipe cleaner together, fastening them just below the flower.

Make as many of these as you need for a bunch—or just the one!

Edible craft activities

Savoury flower

You will need (per child):
- Lettuce leaves
- 1 slice of brown bread
- 1 slice of white bread
- 1 slice of cheese
- 1 slice of carrot
- Celery
- Flower cutters of different sizes

First, chop or rip the lettuce into shreds and arrange on a plate. This will be the lawn for the flowers.

With the largest flower cutter, cut a flower shape from the brown bread.

With the next largest, cut a flower shape from the centre

of the brown bread flower. This can be tricky for younger children, as you need to get the flower cutter in the middle of the bread flower.

Using the same size cutter, cut a flower from the white bread.

Put the smaller white flower into the gap in the brown bread flower.

Repeat using an even smaller flower cutter and the slice of cheese.

If you have enough different sized cutters, you can repeat using a slice of carrot.

Arrange the flower on the lettuce.

Cut a length of celery, splitting it if necessary, and arrange as a stalk.

You can make further flowers as you wish.

Sweet flower

You will need (per child):
- 1 fairy cake
- Buttercream icing
- Green food colouring
- Green fondant icing
- 1 round jelly sweet (for the flower head, so choose carefully which sort of sweet you need)
- 1 short lollipop stick (you can get these from Lakeland or Hobbycraft)
- Knife for spreading

Mix the buttercream icing with green food colouring to make a grass colour.

Spread the fairy cake with the green icing as grass.

Roll out the green fondant icing, and cut some leaves from it.

Spear the jelly sweet with the lollipop stick.

Put the flower into the fairy cake, and arrange the leaves round the base of the stick.

*

Palm Sunday

Suggested Bible passages

Old Testament: Isaiah 50:4–9a

It is the Lord God who helps me; who will declare me guilty?

ISAIAH 50:9A

New Testament: Mark 11:1–11

Then those who went ahead and those who followed were shouting, 'Hosanna! Blessed is the one who comes in the name of the Lord!'

MARK 11:9

Reflection for leaders

Part of my work within the parish is to help the staff of the local church school with their assemblies. Initially I tried to tell stories that were related to the theme of school, and the value that was being explored, such as integrity or friendship.

However, after consultation with the head teacher, it was decided that I should concentrate on telling some of the classic Bible stories that were an essential part not only of a child's Christian spiritual development, but of their cultural understanding as well.

Accordingly I began at the beginning, with Adam and Eve, and started to work my way chronologically through the Old Testament. Every fortnight I told a story and then reflected on its message for us today as Christians. Initially nervous as to how some of the bloodthirsty stories would translate, as time went on I got into my stride and my stories became more dramatic, and my subjects more adventurous. They also became more challenging for me: what is the Christian message implicit in the story of Jacob's deception of Esau, and how can we apply what we learn from this story to our lives today?

As I related the stories of Balaam, Deborah, Jeremiah and Miriam, this simplicity of purpose became ever clearer. Equally clear was the single outstanding message that I shared week after week with the schoolchildren. Every story told of the frailty of human beings; their flaws, their habit of doing the wrong thing whenever the opportunity presented itself. Equally, every story told of the majestic nature of God's people when they rose to the challenges that God put before them; the wonderful things that were accomplished in his name for the good of his people. Every story told of the never-failing love of God for his fragile, damaged children, who constantly strayed from the covenant relationship, testing it to its limits and beyond, incurring God's anger and punishment on occasions, yet never cutting themselves off completely from his forgiveness and grace.

Our Bible is a wonderful resource, packed with every

human emotion that has been experienced, filled with happiness and sorrow, excitement and despair. In the Psalms can be found poems that echo both the joy of Christian living and its challenges, making it a book to turn to at many different moments of our lives. The Old Testament offers adventure and tragedy, journeys and promises, while the New Testament not only tells the story of the Messiah but follows the lives of ordinary people trying to live out their Christian faith in a difficult and hostile world. The most widely sold book in the world, translated into hundreds of languages, the Bible remains something precious and full of promise, a guidebook for us all.

The story of Palm Sunday marks the beginning of Holy Week, the most important and emotionally draining week of the Christian year. Here can be found all the elements of a good story: the mystery of the donkey's availability, the excitement of the procession, the unwary happiness of the disciples, all held in tension by our own knowledge and dark forebodings within the passage that this is just the deceptively joyful beginning of a dark and frightening story—a story with the most incredible ending!

Bible story

Jesus and his friends went on to Jerusalem by way of Bethphage on the Mount of Olives. Jesus asked two of his disciples to go ahead and bring back a young donkey which would be waiting for them.

'If anyone asks what you are doing, tell them I need it, and they will not stop you.'

The two friends did as Jesus asked. They found the young

donkey, and brought it to Jesus. They put a cloak on the back of the animal, which had never yet been ridden. Then Jesus sat on its back and started to ride towards Jerusalem.

'I wonder…'

I wonder if the disciples believed that they would find a donkey…
I wonder how Jesus felt when he saw the crowd waiting to meet him…
I wonder what it was like to be part of the crowd…
I wonder what it would be like to be leading a procession like that…
I wonder what Jesus' enemies felt when they saw how popular he was…

Prayer activity

Find as many different versions of the Bible as you can. You need at least five. These should vary from a book of Bible stories for very young children, through a version suitable for an older child, to a King James Version of the Bible and a modern translation.

Place bookmarks in the following places:

- Genesis 2:1–3 (Creation)
- Exodus 18:8 (Moses)
- 1 Samuel 17:47 (David and Goliath)
- Luke 19:8 (Zacchaeus)
- Matthew 28:5–6 (Easter)

Show the different Bibles to the children. Explain that they all tell the same stories in different ways.

Talk to the children about the Bible being somewhere we can find all that we need to live a Christian life, and a place where we can find lots of different ways to help us to pray.

One by one, pick up the bookmarked Bibles and read the relevant verse or show the illustration.

After each story, pause to allow the children to think about the story. Ask them what sort of prayer they could say using the story.

The Bible shows us that God created everything and that he loves everything that he made.
The Bible shows us that whatever happens in our lives, God will always be with us.
The Bible shows us how we can turn to God when we need courage.
The Bible shows us that God forgives us if we are sorry.
The Bible shows us that we can trust in God for ever.

At the end of the prayer activity, say a prayer together thanking God for all the stories he has given us.

Craft activities

Paper palm leaf

You will need:
- Large green stiff paper
- Pencils
- Scissors

- Coloured pens or crayons
- Foam letters (optional)

From the large green paper, cut an oval shape that ends with a short 'stalk' at one end. Children can copy one already made, or the leaves can be cut out beforehand.

Fold the leaf in half and draw sloping lines from the outside edge towards the centre. These lines should not go all the way to the centre but only about one-third of the way in.

Cut carefully along these lines.

When the leaf has been opened out again, gently separate the leaves or curl them slightly so that they look like fronds on palm branches.

Write 'Hosanna' down the centre spine of the leaf as colourfully and elaborately as possible, or stick the word on in foam letters.

Peat pot donkey

You will need (per child):
- 2 peat pots, one larger than the other (sizes depending on what you can find and on how big your craft sticks are)
- Washable PVA glue
- 2 craft sticks, either ordinary or jumbo size depending on the size of your peat pots
- About 2 m of brown wool
- Stick-on eyes (optional)
- Black marker pen
- Brown card or foam
- Scissors

Peat pots can be bought very cheaply at garden centres. If you have only a small number of children, you can use some peat pots for the 'flower pot' craft on Mothering Sunday

Place the larger peat pot upside down on your work area.

Glue the side of the small peat pot on to the top of the larger peat pot, so that the rim of the small pot is level with part of the rim of the larger one. The small pot thus forms the donkey's head.

Cut the craft sticks in half, and colour the rounded ends brown to form hooves.

Glue two craft sticks to the underside of the large peat pot so that it looks as if the donkey is sitting on his back legs.

Glue the other two sticks to the front of the large peat pot so that the 'hooves' rest on the ground in front of it.

For most children, it will be necessary to prepare this beforehand. It is easiest and quickest with a glue gun as the legs need to be quite robustly fastened on.

Cut ear shapes from the foam or card and glue them to the side of the donkey's head. Stick or draw eyes on either side of the head, and draw two nostrils on the end of the small peat pot as a nose.

To make the mane, cut about eight pieces of brown wool about 24 cm long, and tie them together with another piece of wool about 8 cm from one end. Glue the tied area to the edge of the small peat pot, letting the shorter ends of the wool fall to the front between the ears, and the longer ends down the back of the donkey. You can give the donkey a haircut if needed.

Edible craft activities

Savoury Bible

You will need (per child):
- 3 pieces of bread
- Tortilla (optional)
- 2 pieces of processed cheese or ham
- Squirty mayonnaise or a tube of tomato puree
- Icing bag and fine nozzle (optional)

Cut the crusts from two of the slices of bread and place them side by side on a plate or tortilla.

Cut a strip the length of the crustless slices and about 2 cm wide from the third piece of bread.

Place this strip on the join of the two bread slices—this is the spine of the book.

Cut the cheese or ham to fit the bread book covers, leaving a margin of about 1 cm all the way round.

Using the mayonnaise or tomato puree, draw or write on the pages of the Bible. You can use an icing bag and fine nozzle for this, if available.

Alternatively, you can make a closed Bible by sandwiching the cheese or ham between the two slices of bread and sticking the spine on with mayonnaise. You can then decorate the cover of the Bible with an outline and a cross.

Sweet Bible

You will need (per child):
- 1 fig roll (ideally the sort that are smooth both sides, rather than the ones with ridges)
- White writing icing
- Small amount of red fondant icing
- Rolling pin
- 1 digestive biscuit (optional)
- Blue fondant icing (optional)
- Yellow writing icing (optional)

Using the white writing icing, carefully outline the top and one side of the fig roll so that it looks like the cover of a book. In the centre of the front, draw a small white cross (or write 'Bible' if you are very skilled).

With the red fondant icing, make a long thin strip as a bookmark.

Make a small hole in the fig filling at the bottom of the book and push one end of the bookmark into it.

To make the craft more lengthy (and challenging), you can place the Bible on a 'stand'.

Roll out the blue fondant icing and cut a circle the same size as the digestive biscuit.

Place the icing circle on the biscuit and then the Bible on top.

Decorate the blue icing with yellow writing icing stars or crosses.

*

Maundy Thursday

Theme: Communion

Place/object within the church building: chalice and paten

Suggested Bible passages

Old Testament: Exodus 12:1–14

This day shall be a day of remembrance for you. You shall celebrate it as a festival to the Lord; throughout your generations you shall observe it as a perpetual ordinance.

EXODUS 12:14

New Testament: Luke 22:14–20

Then he took a loaf of bread, and when he had given thanks, he broke it and gave it to them, saying, 'This is my body, which is given for you. Do this in remembrance of me.'

LUKE 2:19

Reflection for leaders

When it comes to food, we are a nation under siege. Daily we are subject to countless messages concerning food. Magazines and newspapers show delicious recipes from celebrity chefs on one page, and on the very next page the latest diet to ensure you shed all those unwanted pounds. Supermarkets groan with shelves full of endless varieties of the same basic necessities. Do you want brown bread or white, seeded, rye, sourdough, bloomer, organic, wholemeal? When we have bought it, we take it home and throw away, on average, about one-third of it. Our relationship with food is fraught and often unhealthy.

Maundy Thursday, in its beautiful simplicity of bread and wine shared among friends, gives us the chance to take back the grace of food and make it once more a life-giving substance to be appreciated in gratitude.

One of the basic facts about food is that you cannot survive without it, however much you think it might simplify your life if you did! It must be taken at regular intervals if you are to benefit properly from it. Eating alone is not nearly as beneficial as eating with other people. Eating with other people reinforces community, encourages good habits and affirms relationships.

When Jesus decided to spend his last night on earth sharing a meal with his closest friends and, in doing so, setting the pattern for the worship of the Church, he really knew what he was doing. At the Last Supper, Jesus did what he had been doing throughout his ministry—he took something earthly and added an unearthly dimension, and in the process enabled us to participate in the meal and the mystery, the community and the communion. The bread and the wine with which we celebrate Jesus' life, death and resurrection create more than a memorial meal; it is a meal that brings life in all its fullness. This meal causes us to remain in Christ and he in us.

Jesus said to them, 'Very truly I tell you, unless you eat the flesh of the Son of Man and drink his blood, you have no life in you. Those who eat my flesh and drink my blood have eternal life, and I will raise them up on the last day' (John 6:53–54).

But there is more. Participation in the Eucharist, the Lord's Supper, Holy Communion, call it what we will, is not only participation in the holy mystery of Christ, but a participation, a joining together with everyone else who does the same thing, both those with us in our own church and those in churches around the world, today and in days gone past, right back to that very first occasion when bread was first taken, broken and shared. The bread we eat, the wine we share makes us one. Christ died so that we could be one, with him in eternity.

Maundy Thursday celebrates our oneness with Christ and with each other. It reminds us of the beauty and sacredness of ordinary things, and cautions us to treat them with care and reverence. It brings together the most disparate, scattered groups of people from all corners of the world and enfolds us all in one great, sacrificial love.

Bible story

Then Jesus held the loaf of unleavened bread and thanked God for it. He broke it into pieces and shared it with his friends.

'Eat this. This is my body which is given for you,' he said. 'Remember me whenever you eat bread together.' Then Jesus picked up a cup of red wine. 'Drink this. This wine is my blood, shed for you so that your sins may be forgiven.'

Jesus' friends ate and drank with him, but they did not understand what Jesus was telling them until after he had died.

'I wonder...'

I wonder what the disciples thought would happen at supper...
I wonder what they felt when Jesus told them the bread was his body...
I wonder how Peter felt...
I wonder what Judas was thinking...
I wonder what the disciples did afterwards...

Prayer activity

You will need:
• 5 types of bread that all taste very different (you could choose rye, sliced white, seeded, pitta bread and a wheat tortilla)

Cut the bread up into small pieces so that there is enough for each child to have a piece of each bread, and place the bread into five different baskets.

Have a bread tasting session. If the children are old enough, you could blindfold them, and they could try to work out what each bread was. If the children are young, then just trying different types of bread will be enough.

At the end of the tasting session, spend some time talking about the different types and which type was preferred. Then introduce the idea that, although they all tasted different, they were all bread. Explain that just as we are all different, we are also all God's children. When we gather for worship together, we become one body, particularly when we eat the bread at the Eucharist (use the word used in your church). We remember the last meal that Jesus had on earth with his disciples, and are thankful that he died so that we could be one with him and with all who worship him.

If there is bread left over, put it all on one plate. Pass the plate from child to child, with each child giving the person next to them a piece of bread, saying, 'You are God's child and he loves you,' as they do so.

At the end, thank God for every member of the church.

Craft activities

Shoebox scene

You will need:
- At least 2 shoeboxes
- Stiff white card
- Washable PVA glue
- Crayons or felt pens
- White cloth or thin white paper
- Scissors
- Air-dry clay or salt dough (optional)

Depending on the number of children in the activity group, glue two or more shoeboxes end to end. Cover them with white cloth or white paper to look like a tablecloth.

Cut out 'gingerbread men' style figures out of the white

card: 13 plus the number of children there are in the group. Alternatively, you can provide a template for the children to draw around and cut out for themselves.

Decorate the first 13 figures to look like Jesus and the twelve disciples. Write their names across their chests: Peter, Andrew, James, John, Philip, Bartholomew, Thomas, Matthew, James, Simon, Thaddaeus, Judas.

Glue these figures along one side of the fabric-covered shoeboxes, putting Jesus in the centre.

With the other figures, invite the children to colour them in to look like themselves, or each other. Write their names across their chests.

Glue these figures around the shoebox, continuing on from the disciples.

If there is time, the children can make miniature plates and drinking vessels from the clay or salt dough.

Plate grace

You will need (per child):
- 1 piece of A3 card or thick paper
- Washable PVA glue
- 1 paper plate
- 1 set of plastic cutlery
- Either sponges for printing, cut in the shape of fruit and vegetables or other food, or peppers, apples, potatoes cut in half
- Poster paints
- Felt pens
- Foam letters (optional)

First, decorate the A3 card or paper with prints of food, either using real food or the sponges.

When these are dry, write a grace along the top of the sheet. This can be simply 'Thank you for our food', or a drawing of some food with 'Amen' underneath, or a lengthier grace, depending on the age of the children. The grace can be traditional or the children can make one up themselves. If you want a traditional grace, it is best to write one out for the children to copy. 'For food and friends, God's name be praised' or 'For what we are about to receive may the Lord make us truly thankful' or 'Bless this bunch as we munch our lunch' are some suggestions. You could also use foam letters to stick on the words of a grace.

The edge of the plate can be decorated with patterns if there is time.

When the painting is dry, glue the paper plate on to the A3 paper, with the cutlery arranged either side. This will take a while to dry, so do not try and lift it until you are sure the cutlery is thoroughly stuck.

Edible craft activities

Savoury disciples' boat

You will need (per child):
- 1 tortilla
- 2 slices of salami
- 2 cheese slices
- 1 olive
- 1 pitta bread
- 1 stick of celery

Cut the pitta bread about one-third along, and place on the tortilla as the hull of the boat.

Slice the olive and place the pieces on the pitta as portholes.

Cut one of the cheese slices into a smaller square as the little sail.

Make two holes in each of the sails and thread a piece of celery stick through as masts.

Cut thin crescents from the salami and arrange around the boat as waves.

Sweet disciples' boat

You will need (per child):
- Blue jelly (use lemon jelly with blue food colouring added if you cannot find any blue jelly)
- 1 slice of melon
- 2 cocktail sticks
- 2 slices of kiwi fruit
- 1 grape

Chop up the jelly and arrange in a bowl as the sea.

Put the melon on to the jelly as the boat.

Slice the kiwi fruit into two thin slices.

Slice the grape in half.

Put a slice of kiwi and a grape half on each cocktail slice as sails and flags.

＊

Good Friday

Theme: Jesus' sacrifice for us; our offering of ourselves in his service

Place/object within the church building: cross

Suggested Bible passages

Old Testament: Isaiah 52:13—53:12

But he was wounded for our transgressions, crushed for our iniquities; upon him was the punishment that made us whole, and by his bruises are we healed.
ISAIAH 53:5

New Testament: Mark 15:33–40

Then Jesus gave a loud cry and breathed his last.
MARK 15:37

Reflection for leaders

There is no escaping the brutality of the crucifixion, just as there is no escaping the fact that at the centre of our faith lies the cross as well as the empty tomb, and that before Easter Day can be celebrated, we must experience Good

Friday. This is perhaps the most difficult of festivals to share with children. Although the details of a death upon a cross might hold a sort of grim fascination, the danger is that this will capture the imagination more strongly than the reasons behind the death of Christ—that of a vast, powerful love so rich and deep that even death cannot defeat it. Perhaps the emphasis should be less on the physical suffering of Christ upon the cross and more upon his sacrifice, his willingness to give everything he had, including his life, for those whom he loved. Our living out of our faith must be like that as well—no half measures. Time and again Jesus asks for all of us, not just the part that we feel happy giving:

'When Jesus heard this, he said to him, "There is still one thing lacking. Sell all that you own and distribute the money to the poor, and you will have treasure in heaven; then come, follow me"' (Luke 18:22); 'Love the Lord your God with all your heart, and with all your soul, and with all your mind, and with all your strength' (Mark 12:30); and, scariest of all, 'Love your neighbour as yourself' (v. 31).

It is a bit embarrassing, really, in our carefully limited world, to have so much asked of us. If our response to the gospel message is to be at all true and honest, this is how it must be. A Christian life is all-embracing, all-encompassing; it cannot be something that is observed from the sidelines. Such a great love as Christ showed to each and every one of us demands in return a willingness to respond with a wholeheartedness that knows no limits. This is not easy. To be fair, we were never promised that living the Christian life would be easy, but only that Jesus would always be with us, in front of us, by our side, guarding our backs, continually encouraging us as he journeys alongside us, always with the knowledge that because of his death we need fear death no more. However dark and dangerous the journey, however difficult parts of our lives may be, we have been redeemed by the one who made the final sacrifice for us, so that we did not have to. In the face of such a great love, what can we do but respond ourselves with love?

Bible story

The route was lined with people. Some shouted and jeered; others watched sadly; yet more wept and cried to see Jesus taken away to Golgotha, the Place of the Skull.

Two other men were led out to be crucified that day, both of them thieves. Jesus was nailed to the wooden bar and hoisted up between them.

'Forgive them, Father!' said Jesus. 'They don't know what they are doing!' The crowds watched and waited. The soldiers jeered.

'You saved other people, but you can't help yourself!' they said.

Some of the soldiers gambled for Jesus' clothes. Others made a sign to hang over his head.

'This is the King of the Jews,' it said.

At midday the sky turned black. At around three o'clock in the afternoon, Jesus called out loud, 'It is finished!' and breathed his last breath.

'I wonder...'

I wonder what Jesus' mother felt as she saw Jesus on the cross...

I wonder why the soldiers laughed at him...

I wonder how the crowd felt when the sky turned black...

I wonder what the disciples felt when they saw that Jesus had died...

I wonder why Jesus wanted God to forgive the people who had killed him...

Prayer activity

You will need:
- Large bowl filled with nails
- Smaller bowl filled with self-adhesive foam hearts
- Large cut-out cross or drawing of a cross (big enough for each child to stick on a heart, so will depend on the size of your group)

Place the cross at one end of your prayer circle so that everyone can see it. At its foot put an empty bowl and a bowl full of foam hearts.

Place the bowl of nails in the centre of your circle. Tell the children that today we think about the death of Jesus, how he loved each one of us so much that he was prepared to be punished for the things we had done wrong so that we did not have to suffer.

In as much detail as the age and understanding of the children allows, ask the group to take one nail out of the bowl for each of the following things that we might do wrong:

- Pride—thinking we are better than other people, or showing off in front of others
- Selfishness—taking more than we need, or grabbing before others can get there

- Lack of courage—when we have not stood up for what we know is right
- Anger—saying or doing things to hurt other people.

Ask them to hold these four nails in their hands and in silence say sorry for all the times they have been proud, selfish, cowardly or hurt other people.

Finally, ask the children to put the nails in the bowl at the foot of the cross and stick a heart on to the cross as a sign that they know they have been forgiven for the things they have done wrong, and that Jesus' love is for them and for all people.

Craft activities

Peg cross

You will need (per child):
- 8 clothes pegs
- Cardboard
- Strong glue or glue gun
- Acrylic paint
- Washable PVA glue
- Decorations such as buttons and sequins (optional)

Separate the clothes pegs from the metal spring.

Glue the single peg parts together in groups of three, with the thick ends together and the thin ends together.

Lay them together to form a cross. The thin ends of the pegs should be facing the outward ends of the cross.

Using this shape as a guide, draw a cross-shaped template from the card. This only needs to be done once, as you can then draw more card bases from the one template.

Cut out the card cross base.

Glue the pegs on to the base with strong glue or a glue gun.

Paint with acrylic paint mixed with PVA glue.

While the paint is still damp, you can stick sequins or other decorations on to the cross. You can paint the cross in just one colour and leave it undecorated if you prefer.

St Brigid's cross

This craft needs some dexterity and is not really suitable for young children. You could make up the pipe cleaner crosses beforehand and provide strips of brightly coloured fabric that could be woven among the strands of the cross.

St Brigid was a very wise and gifted nun, who lived in the fifth century in Ireland. She founded a convent and a monastery and was renowned for her care for the poor and the sick. There is a story which tells of her nursing a sick king of one of the local tribes. As she sat by his bedside, when the fever got very bad, she watched and waited and prayed for him. While she was praying, she picked up some of the rushes that covered the floor of the room where he lay and began to weave them into a cross shape. The king, sick and in pain, asked her what she was doing, and Brigid told him the story of Jesus. As he listened, the king felt himself grow well and strong. By the time he was better, he was a convert to Christianity. His tribe also became followers of Christ and, by doing so, ended years of conflict in that region.

You will need (per child):
- 8 pipe cleaners

First, bend all of the pipe cleaners in half.

Take the first pipe cleaner and hold it so that the ends are pointing to the left. Hook the next pipe cleaner through the first so that it points towards you, making sure they meet where they bend. Hook the third pipe cleaner in to the second, but this time so that the points are towards the right. Then add a fourth, pointing upwards. This will be the foundation of the cross, with the four bends of the pipe cleaners interwoven in the middle. Continue to add more pipe cleaners in the same order (with the points facing left, down, right, up) until they are all used. When you have finished, twist the ends together so that they stay in place.

Edible craft activities

Savoury crown of thorns

You will need:
- 1 bagel (optional)
- Twiglets®
- Squirty cheese

Slice the bagel, if you are using it, in two horizontally.

Spread one half of the bagel thickly with squirty cheese.

Arrange the Twiglets in a circle to look like a crown of thorns, sticking them together using the squirty cheese. You can arrange them on the bagel or on a plate.

Sweet crown of thorns

You will need:
- Box of stick biscuits (Mikado biscuits are excellent; alternatively, use large Matchmakers chocolates, or straight pretzels if you don't mind salty and sweet mixed together)
- Half a bar of chocolate for melting
- Baking paper

First, draw a circle on the baking paper. Make it the size you want the crown of thorns to be. It helps if you then draw a smaller circle inside the larger one, giving a good guide as to where the thorns will go.

Melt the chocolate in a microwave, if you have one, or by stirring it in a bowl over a saucepan of barely simmering water (see Recipes section). If your church is not equipped with a stove, use boiling water from a kettle and keep topping it up with more boiling water.

You now need to coat the biscuits with chocolate. You can do this by tipping the biscuits into the melted chocolate and stirring very carefully, trying not to break the biscuits.

Alternatively, if you have a number of children all doing the activity, keep the biscuits and chocolate separate and provide scrupulously clean paint brushes for the children to dip into the melted chocolate and then paint on to the biscuits. The biscuits do not have to be completely coated—they look better if they are slightly patchy and rough.

When the biscuits are covered in chocolate, arrange them on the baking paper, gradually building up a wreath shape as you go. Take care to arrange the biscuits so that they stick out in many different directions, like thorns.

Let the crown of thorns set firmly before taking it off the baking paper, but be careful, as it will still be a very fragile construction.

Since eating chocolate on Good Friday might be felt inappropriate, you could keep the crown of thorns until Easter Day. Then fill it with chocolate eggs, turning it from a crown of thorns into a nest of eggs!

✳

Easter

Theme: God's love for all people

Place/object within the church building: altar

Suggested Bible passages

Old Testament: Isaiah 25:6–9

He will swallow up death forever. Then the Lord God will wipe away the tears from all faces, and the disgrace of his people he will take away from all the earth, for the Lord has spoken.

ISAIAH 25:8

New Testament: Mark 16:1–8

So they went out and fled from the tomb, for terror and amazement had seized them; and they said nothing to anyone for they were afraid.

MARK 16:8

Reflection for leaders

I leave it to be settled by whomsoever it may concern whether the tendency of this work be altogether to recommend parental tyranny or reward filial disobedience.

JANE AUSTEN, *Northanger Abbey*

Come children, let us shut up the box and the puppets, for our play is played out.

WILLIAM THACKERAY, *Vanity Fair*

But Flopsy, Mopsy and Cottontail had bread and milk and blackberries for supper.

BEATRIX POTTER, *The Tale of Peter Rabbit*

For they were afraid.

THE GOSPEL ACCORDING TO MARK

What a strange way to end a story—well, nearly end, because research that has been done on the text has concluded that the Gospel as written by St Mark actually ends here and that the rest of the chapter up to the end was added on later. For the moment, let us look at this as the ending, and compare it to the other endings above. The difference is obvious. For the first three endings are profoundly satisfactory. Having tied up any loose ends, the book ends with a bit of moralising or a romantic fade-out. In any case, the reader is well aware that the end of the book has been reached. But what about the Gospel?

Mark's Gospel is without doubt a carefully crafted and dramatically satisfying story—Jesus is sharply proclaimed as Lord and Christ, the disciples muddle along wrongheaded and unbelieving, and then it ends abruptly with the words 'for they were afraid'.

What sort of ending is this? The resurrection has just happened; God's plan for the salvation of the world has begun; the disciples, who only hours before were in the depth of sadness and despair, have had their hopes reignited... and then it ends. It doesn't make sense! It unsettles us as we have nowhere to rest. It is not surprising that later readers of this Gospel began to supply their own endings, something that wrapped things up nicely, that satisfied their need for finality, for a proper ending. What was added was, after all, the truth—that the resurrection of Jesus inspired new life in his followers—but it does make Mark's Gospel a completely different book. The added ending makes the Gospel into a conventional story that can be safely left while the reader returns to their own world and time. Mark's Gospel, ending as it does—'and they were afraid'—does not leave the reader in peace. We are unsettled, left off balance, with a decision to make as to where to go next. Will the reader come down on the side of belief or unbelief? What will the conclusion to the story be? It is as if the writer steps aside at the last moment and puts the pen into our hands, the hands of every single one of us, and asks us to write the conclusion with our own words, our own actions, our own lives.

Bible story

Mary Magdalene wanted to anoint Jesus' body with spices. She went early on Sunday morning so that she could be there at sunrise.

When she arrived in the garden, she saw that the huge stone that had been in front of the tomb had been rolled away. The tomb was empty.

Mary ran back to find Peter and John.

'They've taken Jesus away!' she cried. 'I don't know where his body is!'

Peter and John ran to the tomb to see if there could be any mistake. They saw the linen cloths, but Jesus was not there.

The two men ran home, leaving Mary alone in the garden.

Mary was still weeping when she went to look inside the tomb again. But this time she saw two angels, sitting where Jesus' body should have been.

'Why are you crying?' asked one of the angels.

'They have taken my master away,' Mary sobbed. 'I don't know where they have put him!'

Mary turned as she heard someone else behind her. She thought it was the gardener.

'Who are you looking for?' the man asked.

'Please just tell me where his body is,' she said.

The man answered with just one word.

'Mary!' he said. Mary knew straight away who the man was. It was Jesus!

'Master!' she said, overjoyed to see him.

'Don't touch me,' he said to her gently, 'but go and tell the others what you have seen.'

Mary ran all the way.

'I have seen Jesus!' she said. 'He's no longer dead. He's alive!'

'I wonder...'

I wonder how Mary felt on her way to the tomb...

I wonder if Mary recognised that the people were angels...

I wonder why Mary thought the man was the gardener...

I wonder how Mary felt when she realised that the man was Jesus...

I wonder what I would say if it had happened to me...

Prayer activity

You will need:
- A large deep flower pot, filled with bulb compost
- Pictures of flowers, enough for each child
- Double-sided tape
- Bulbs, ideally one for each child (narcissus bulbs are relatively cheap, and if purchased near Easter time will probably be on special offer)

Place the flower pot in the middle of the prayer circle and a basket filled with the bulbs to one side. Ask the children to imagine what it is like in the middle of the flower pot. It must be very dark as there will be no light at all reaching the centre. You would not be able to see or hear anyone. It would probably be uncomfortable.

Ask the children to plant the bulbs, burying them deep in the compost. It seems like this is the wrong thing to do, to take the bulbs out of the warmth and the light and put them into somewhere dark and damp. Tell the children that this is what the disciples felt like after Jesus had died. They felt as if they had been out in the sunshine but that all the light had been taken away from them. They were lonely and afraid.

Remind the children that some times in our lives seem very dark. We are unhappy about things, or frightened about the future. It can seem as if we will never be happy again.

However, even as the bulbs are in the ground, they are growing and changing. Soon their shoots will appear out of the top of the pot and then they will grow upwards, rejoicing in the heat and the light of the sun. Their beauty will bring joy to everyone who sees them.

Jesus had to die so that he could break down the barriers that had been built between human beings and God. Even at the darkest time, just after his death, he was preparing for his resurrection. Jesus' resurrection means that none of us have to stay in the dark, but that we can all live in the light, as his love is always with us.

The disciples were filled with joy when they saw Jesus. They knew they did not have to be afraid again.

Ask the children to decorate the outside of the flower pot with pictures of flowers as a reminder that even though the flowers cannot be seen, they are loved by God and growing towards the light.

If the children are old enough, you can read them these words that were found scratched on a wall in a concentration camp in World War II:

'I believe in the sun when it is not shining. I believe in love when I do not feel it. I believe in God, even when he is silent.'

Craft activities

Easter garden

You will need (per child):
- 1 large saucer as a plant pot (available quite cheaply from a garden centre)
- Potting compost
- A handful of stones or pebbles
- 6 small craft sticks
- Brown acrylic paint or felt pens
- Grass seed or cress seed
- Large tray (optional)

Preparation

Buy the saucer in a size in proportion to the size of the children you are working with; don't make them so big that the children cannot handle them easily or safely, but they need to be deep enough to support the crosses.

Before the craft activity, make three crosses out of the craft sticks. They will need to be quite robust as they will be subject to watering, so, if possible, stick them together with a glue gun.

It is most effective if you tip the compost into a large shallow tray for the children to work with. I use one of those plastic storage drawers that go underneath beds as they are a good size and depth.

Paint or colour the crosses and put them aside to dry.

Fill the plant pot saucers with compost and then arrange the stones and crosses to make a garden in whatever design you want. Some older children may want to build a tomb structure; younger ones may be content just to put the crosses in.

When the garden is complete, sprinkle the soil with grass or cress seed. Grass seed looks more authentic, but cress grows very quickly and has the added advantage of being able to be harvested and eaten.

'Easter egg' balloon

You will need:
- 1 ball of crochet cotton (needs to be 100 per cent cotton)
- 1 bottle of fabric stiffening solution (you can get this from John Lewis, which sells it for making roller blinds)
- 1 balloon
- Feathers, ribbons, sequins and other decorations
- Baking paper (optional)

Preparation

Make up the fabric stiffening solution according to the instructions.

Blow up the balloon until about half inflated. It should ideally still be egg-shaped but have enough air in to be quite rigid.

Unwind a length of crochet cotton and soak it in the fabric stiffening solution.

Wrap the cotton around the balloon so that it forms a sort of net around the balloon. Squeeze the excess liquid from the cotton as you go, or it will take forever to dry.

Continue to soak lengths of cotton and wrap them round the balloon until you have a structure. It can have gaps between the threads, but it must look as if it will be self-supporting. Hang up or leave on baking paper until absolutely dry.

When dry, pop the balloon. The thread should now form a hollow ball that can be decorated by winding things in among the threads or sticking things on to them.

Edible craft activities

Savoury Easter basket

You will need (per child):
- 1 pitta bread
- 1 slice of processed cheese
- 1 slice of ham
- Egg-shaped biscuit cutter
- Lettuce leaves (optional)
- Knife for cutting
- Icing nozzle or very small icing cutters

Cut out a semicircle from one end of the pitta bread, taking care not to break the edges. This then makes a basket shape, complete with handle.

Gently ease away the two layers of pitta bread at the top of the basket.

Cut out an egg shape from the ham and cheese slices.

With the scraps from the edge, cut out small circles. You can use the end of an icing nozzle to do this, unless you have very small icing cutters.

Using the same cutter, cut out shapes from the ham and cheese eggs.

Carefully put the two eggs into the pitta basket, gently tucking the ends in between the layers of pitta.

Once the eggs are in the basket, fill in the holes you have cut out, using contrasting circles of cheese and ham.

Place the basket on a bed of lettuce leaves if you wish.

Sweet Easter biscuits

You will need:
- Double quantity of biscuit dough
- Egg-shaped cookie cutter
- Very small circular cutter (you could use the end of an icing nozzle for this) or similar small shape
- Writing icing in as many different colours as you have

Preparation

Roll out the biscuit dough and cut out double the number of egg-shaped biscuits you will need for each child.

From half the biscuits, cut out small circles, stars or flower shapes, depending on the number of small cutters you have.

Bake the biscuits as per the recipe on page 29.

Take two biscuits per craft.

On the whole biscuit, spread patches of different coloured writing icing. Make the icing patches quite thick.

Place the biscuit with the holes cut out on top of the whole biscuit. Push down firmly so that the writing icing squishes through the holes.

*

$\mathcal{A}$scension

Theme: the Christian journey

Place/object within the church building: nave

Suggested Bible passages

Old Testament: Daniel 7:9–14

As I watched in the night visions, I saw one like a human being coming with the clouds of heaven.
DANIEL 7:13A

New Testament: Luke 24:50–53

While he was blessing them, he withdrew from them and was carried up into heaven.
LUKE 24:51

Reflection for leaders

In recent years, pilgrimage—generally defined as 'a spiritual journey to a sacred place'—has grown in popularity once more, with many people making not only the traditionally gruelling long-distance walking trips, but also day-long pilgrimages or pilgrimages by coach. Pilgrimage has a very long history. The Old Testament is full of the journeys made not only by figures such as Moses and Abraham but also by prophets such as Joshua and Ezekiel, leaders such as David, and even ordinary people such as Ruth and Naomi. Christ himself was an itinerant—'the Son of Man has nowhere to lay his head' (Matthew 8:20)—and Christian pilgrimage has its roots in the very early church: almost as soon as Christianity began to be established around the world, people wanted to see the exact places where Christ lived and preached. People journey for adventure, to challenge themselves, to change. They encounter different people, new landscapes, and often gain knowledge about themselves and others that would not have been achieved if they had remained in their home places.

The pilgrimage metaphor serves us well for our faith journey, and for an example of this we return to the nave, the ceiling of which we gazed at during Epiphany, and look again at the journey of the wise men, who set out in faith to discover what event was heralded by the arrival of that great star. They did not know where it would lead them, how long the journey would take or what dangers it might entail. They knew only that it was vital for them to follow the star. They were hoping to witness the arrival of the Messiah, and to their minds, the risks and dangers of the journey were worth that hope. The journey of the wise men does lead them into danger: they encounter Herod, who adds his journey to theirs. But Herod's quest is destined to failure, because no one can make our journeys for us—they have to be personal and wholehearted. It is not enough to know about Jesus; the only true way is to decide to follow him in faith, not knowing where such a journey will lead, only trusting that it will end with an opportunity to worship.

There is a place near the Mount of Olives that tradition holds to bear the footprints made by Christ as he ascended into heaven, the last mark he made upon earth. Jesus' physical journey on earth ended with an admonition to us to continue his work of loving and caring for our neighbours and trusting in God, journeying faithfully onwards in our own quest towards Christ, meeting him along the way in the faces of our fellow travellers.

All journeys begin from home, and pilgrimages return there too, with people changed from their experiences, having learnt much from the journey. The nave is a place of gathering, of coming together for courage before the undertaking of the journey of transformation. It is a resting place, where travellers can seek refreshment on the way, before continuing along a road which will end in a glorious arrival at a new home, transformed by their journey.

Bible story

About six weeks after Jesus rose from the dead, the apostles were with him on the Mount of Olives.

'When the Holy Spirit comes, you will have power,' Jesus said. 'The whole world will hear about me, because you will tell them. You will be my messengers.'

Then Jesus was covered by a cloud and seemed to rise up and disappear while they stood and stared.

Jesus had gone.

'What are you looking for?' asked two angels, standing among them. 'Jesus has gone back to heaven, but one day he will return.'

'I wonder...'

I wonder what the place of the Ascension looked like...
I wonder what the disciples thought would happen...
I wonder what the disciples saw when Jesus was taken up into heaven...
I wonder how they felt after Jesus had gone...
I wonder what they did next...

Prayer activity

You will need:
• Template of the outline of a bare foot
• Lots of pieces of paper
• Scissors

Preparation

If you do not have a great deal of time, you may wish to cut out lots of outlines of feet beforehand. Each child should have at least two, but it would be better if they had anything up to a dozen each.

Take the children to the nave, and ask them to sit on the floor in the middle of the nave. As in the Epiphany prayer activity, remind them that the roof in many churches looks like the bottom of a ship. This is to help us remember that we are all travellers on a journey, that this earth is not our final destination.

Introduce the theme of pilgrimage, describing how from

very earliest times people have wanted to visit places where special things happened. These places were either associated with Jesus, such as Bethlehem or Nazareth, or with saints, such as Santiago de Compostela or Rome. The journeys to these places can take a long time or a short time, and very often have the effect of changing the way we think about things and people.

Explain that our Christian faith is like a journey that takes us to all sorts of places. Lead the children to the font, and explain that our journey as followers of Christ begins with the promises we make or which are made on our behalf, to try to follow the example of Jesus and to obey his commandments to love each other and to love God. In a short time of silence, encourage the children to ask God to bless all those beginning their Christian journey; if there are any who have been recently baptised in the church, pray for them by name. Leave a footprint by the font.

Lead the children back along the nave, towards the altar. If your font is not in a suitable place for this, start at the church door. If you have enough footprints, leave some along the way, and ask the children to think about people who help on their Christian journey, such as teachers and parents. They might like to write those names on the footprints.

At the altar, remind the children that, just like the wise men, who followed the star without knowing where they were going, we too do not know what will happen in our lives or where following God will lead us. But we do have his promise that he will always be with us, journeying alongside us, and that he will meet us at the end.

Place the footprints by the altar and in a time of silence thank God for all the journey companions he sends us, especially Jesus.

Craft activities

Footprints

This is a spectacularly messy craft, and it is best undertaken in a carefree spirit with a willingness to spend quite a lot of time tidying up afterwards.

You will need:
- Lots of space!
- 1 roll of wallpaper lining
- Protective floor covering
- Several different colours of washable paint in flat, shallow bowls (washing-up bowls are best; buckets would do, but they are tricky for children to step in and out of)
- Clean, soapy water
- Towels
- Wellies in various sizes

Unroll the lining paper as far as you have space.

Place the paint bowls at one end and the clean soapy water to one side at the other.

Encourage the children to take off their shoes and socks and make footprints all the way along the paper, washing their feet at the end.

Some children will not have done this before, others only when they were at playgroup, so there may be some hesitation at first. Set an example by doing it yourself. Allow the children time to feel the paint squishing between their toes before they step on to the paper.

Those children who really don't want to get their feet messy can use wellies to make prints, but try not to offer this immediately.

Landscape

You will need:
- A3 piece of stiff paper or card
- Sandpaper
- Green sheets of self-adhesive felt (Hobbycraft are good suppliers of this)
- Brown tissue paper
- Blue fabric
- Collage material (as many different types as you can gather together—scraps of coloured paper, pipe cleaners, beads, fabric, felt, foam, craft sticks and all the oddments left over from other craft activities)
- Strong glue

The object of the craft activity is to make a landscape. This can be done in any way the children wish. Use the basic materials of sandpaper, green felt and brown tissue to make different types of ground, and include a patch of water. Then encourage the children to make flowers from tissue paper, beads and pipe cleaners, and plants from coloured fabric and bits of craft stick. Allow plenty of time for this activity, as it can take some time for the children to realise that there are no instructions and that they must work from their imaginations. Let them play with the materials, arranging them in different ways before finally glueing them to the board. Try not to be too directive about how it is all used!

At the end, you could suggest cutting out a small set of footprints and sticking them along the paper.

Edible craft activities

Savoury landscape

You will need (per child):
- 1 tortilla
- 1 tbsp of rice cooked in water with blue food colouring added (optional)
- 1 tbsp of houmous
- Lettuce
- 1 stick of celery
- 1 head of broccoli
- 1 head of cauliflower
- 3 cm carrot
- Half of each of a red, green and yellow pepper
- Knife for spreading
- Small flower cutter

Using the tortilla as a base, create a landscape using the blue rice as sky, the houmous as a road or path and the lettuce as grass or garden. The broccoli and cauliflower can be made into bushes, and flowers cut out of the carrots and peppers. There is no need to limit yourself just to these foods— anything that is available can be used to construct plants and scenery.

Sweet landscape

You will need (per child):
- 1 large syrup pancake
- 3 digestive biscuits
- 3 Oreo® cookies
- Vanilla buttercream
- Chocolate buttercream
- Mini Smarties®, sprinkles, marshmallows, flower cake decorations

Crush the digestive biscuits into fine crumbs.

Split the Oreo cookies, remove the filling, then crush the cookies into fine crumbs.

Spread a section of the pancake with vanilla buttercream icing. This will be the path, so make it winding and not too wide.

Spread the rest of the pancake with chocolate buttercream icing.

Very carefully, trying not to mix the two together, sprinkle the vanilla icing with crushed digestive biscuit, and the chocolate icing with crushed Oreo biscuit. These will be the garden and a path running through it.

Craft flowers from marshmallows halved and dipped in sprinkles, mini Smarties or flower cake decorations. You can even make a rockery effect by building a pile of marshmallows, stuck together with icing, then sticking flowers on top of them.

*

Pentecost

Theme: sending out of disciples

Place/object within the church building: door

Suggested Bible passages

New Testament: Acts 2:1–47

And suddenly from heaven there came a sound like the rush of a violent wind, and it filled the entire house where they were sitting. Divided tongues, as of fire, appeared among them and a tongue rested on each of them. All of them were filled with the Holy Spirit.

ACTS 2:2–4A

New Testament: Acts 8:26–40

[Philip] asked, 'Do you understand what you are reading?' He replied, 'How can I unless someone guides me?'

ACTS 8:30B–31A

Reflection for leaders

As part of my work as a priest, I visit those who are dying, accompanying them on their last journey on this earth, praying for them and watching with those who love them. I remember one occasion very vividly, when I sat with a woman who had been to church Sunday after Sunday, for the 96 years of her life. She said nothing, hovering as she was in the twilight between life and death. When I began to say the Lord's Prayer out loud, she opened her eyes, her lips moved and she repeated the words with me. This contrasts almost painfully with the fact that when I take a marriage service for a young couple, I now remind them to put the words of the Lord's Prayer in the service sheet, because if they don't, few people can remember them. These two incidents only confirm what we are being told from other sources—the need for people to share the good news of the gospel to a largely unaware world.

The New Testament story of Philip on the road to Gaza has in it two elements that we don't often meet in our daily life nowadays: chariots and eunuchs. Nonetheless, its immediacy, its relevance, practically shout off the page at us. For me, it is one of the most important texts about how to do mission; how to share the news of God's love with the people we meet.

The eunuch is discovered by Philip sitting in his chariot reading Isaiah. The Spirit then says to Philip, 'Go over to this chariot and join it.' So Philip runs to the chariot and asks what the man is reading, and talks to him about it. This is a brave thing to do, but something that we too must undertake. Seekers nowadays do not want or need someone telling them what is what. They need someone to walk alongside them, accompanying them on their journey of discovery. It is vital that all of us talk about our faith. It isn't easy, but if we don't, who will? As Paul writes in his letter to the Romans, 'How then, can they call on one they have not believed in? And how can they believe in the one of whom they have not heard? And how can they hear without someone preaching to them? And how can they preach unless they are sent?' (Romans 10:14–15, NIV).

'Preaching' here does not mean standing up on your soap box or even in your pulpit but living a Christian life. As the famous saying goes, you are the only Bible many people will ever read. At Pentecost we stand shoulder to shoulder with the disciples as they receive their commission to go out into the world and share the news of God's saving love for all people. We know it won't be easy, but the gift of the Holy Spirit means that we will never be alone.

Bible story

Jerusalem was full of visitors from all over the world. They had come for the festival of Pentecost. The believers were together in one room when, suddenly, a sound like a strong wind blew through the house, filling it with noise. Something like flames seemed to burn in the air and touch each person there. As the Holy Spirit touched them, they all began to speak in other languages.

The noise from the house attracted a crowd.

'What's happening?' some of them said. 'I can understand what these men are saying. They are speaking in my language, talking about God. How is this possible?'

'They're drunk!' laughed others.

'No, we're not!' said Peter, coming out to speak to the crowd. 'It's only nine o'clock in the morning.' Then Peter stood up to teach all those who would listen.

First, Peter reminded them of what the prophets had told them would happen. Then he talked to them about Jesus,

God's chosen one, the Messiah. When Peter described how Jesus had been arrested and beaten and then put to death, the people were horrified.

'What shall we do?' they asked.

'You must turn away from your sins and be baptised,' Peter declared. 'Then you can be forgiven, and you will receive the Holy Spirit as we have.'

That day 3000 people became followers of Jesus. The apostles performed many miracles in the name of Jesus, and they met together with the other believers to worship God, to pray and to share what they had with each other.

'I wonder...'

I wonder how the disciples felt before the Holy Spirit came upon them...

I wonder what it feels like to have flames on your head that don't burn...

I wonder how the disciples felt when they spoke different languages...

I wonder how they felt when everyone had gone home...

I wonder what I would say to someone who did not know about Jesus...

Prayer activity

You will need:
- Brown and black paper or thin card, about A4 size
- Tissue paper, brightly coloured paper or lots of different scraps of coloured paper

- Felt pens or marker pens
- Sticky tape
- Glue sticks
- Foam letters or letter stencil
- Scissors

Give each child a piece of black or brown paper and ask them to design a door. If they wish, they can look round the church and copy one of the ones that they can see. Give them lots of opportunity to walk around and draw, or invite them to use the coloured paper and scissors and make a collage door. While they are doing this, talk to them about being the only Bible people read, and ask the children what this might mean. Discuss how living a Christian life gives other people an idea of what Jesus might be like. Discuss the sorts of things they might do that would show people how following Jesus makes you behave.

When all the doors have been created, tape them together to form a giant door shape. On the front, either stencil or use foam letters to spell out the words, 'Send us out in the power of the Spirit.'

If you can, fasten the door patchwork to one of the church doors. (If you are going to do this, measure how big the patchwork needs to be beforehand!)

Gather round the door and pray for an awareness of God's Spirit with us and the grace to show people what God's love means to us.

Craft activities

Kite

Caution: Ornamental—will not fly!

You will need (per child):
- 4 drinking straws (ideally with bendy bits two-thirds along the length of the straw)
- Red and yellow tissue paper
- Scissors
- Thin string or embroidery thread
- Stars or sequins
- Glue sticks
- Sticky tape
- Thread

First, make a square from the drinking straws. They will be most robust if you push one end of the straw into the next straw, then bend them to form a square. Tape round the section where the straws join.

Cut a rectangle of tissue paper that is the size of two of the squares.

Wrap the tissue paper around the kite straws.

Leave to dry.

While this is drying, make three streamers by cutting long strips of tissue paper and decorating with sequins or stars. When the kite is dry, you can decorate it or simply fasten the streamers to the back of the kite, at one of the corners.

Add some thread to the top corner so that you can hang up the kite, letting it blow in the wind.

Pentecost dove

You will need (per child):
- 1 round doily
- Pencil
- Scissors
- Thread

Fold the doily in half, then into quarters.

Open out the doily again into a half, then fold one of the sides in half inwards, so that the edge lines up with the middle crease. Repeat for the other side.

Fold in half again. You should now have a doily that looks like a slice of cake—a triangle with a rounded edge.

With the point upwards and the closed edge to the right, draw a line diagonally from the bottom left-hand edge of the triangle to a point that is about one third along the opposite edge from the point. Mark with your pencil a point that is two thirds along this line from the bottom left-hand edge where it began.

With the scissors, cut from the bottom left-hand edge to your pencil mark.

Hold the doily so that the cut is at the bottom. Fold the wings up on either side of the body, so that the base of the wing forms a horizontal line.

Fold the point of the triangle in and downwards to make a beak.

Fasten a thread to the dove's back and hang it up from the ceiling. Continue making as many as you have doilies until you have a whole flock of doves.

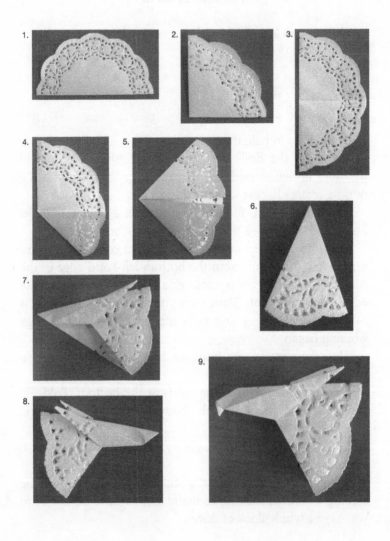

152

Edible craft activities

Savoury flames

You will need (per child):
- 1 scone (see scone recipe on page 31) (alternatively, use thick slices of bread that have been cut into circles)
- Tomato ketchup (if the ketchup is too runny, you can thicken it with some tomato puree; as this has quite a strong taste, don't use too much)
- Cream cheese
- Tortilla chips
- Knife for spreading

Spread the scone thickly with cream cheese.

Break the tortilla chips so that you have just the corners.

Dip the points in tomato ketchup.

Stand the tortilla chips point side up in circles in the cream cheese, so that they look like tongues of fire.

Sweet flames

You will need (per child):
- 1 fairy cake
- 10 mini marshmallows
- Scissors
- Red sugar crystals (available from cake decorating shops or craft stores such as Hobbycraft and Lakeland)

- Vanilla buttercream icing
- Yellow food colouring
- Disposable icing bags

Mix the yellow food colouring with the buttercream icing.

Cut the corner off the disposable icing bag, and fill the bag with the yellow icing. The icing should come out in a sausage shape. Younger children may want to practise making this shape first, using the icing on baking paper.

Cover the fairy cake with a swirl of icing. If you can get it so that the icing makes a small cone shape, that would be very good, but it is not that important. If it all goes wrong, scrape the icing off the cake, put it back in the icing bag and try again.

When the fairy cake has been iced, put to one side.

With the scissors, cut the mini marshmallows diagonally from top to bottom along the longest surface.

Dip the cut end of each half in sugar crystals.

Stand the marshmallows upright in a circle in the centre of the fairy cake, red crystal side pointing outwards.

Put another circle round the outside of the fairy cake to form two circles of flames, ideally with the inner circle higher than the outer, so that it can be seen.

*

Trinity Sunday

Theme: harmony

Place/object within the church building: bells or organ

Suggested Bible passages

Old Testament: Psalm 150

Praise the Lord. Praise God in his sanctuary; praise him in his mighty heavens.

PSALM 150:1, NIV

New Testament: John 16:13–15

When the Spirit of truth comes, he will guide you into all the truth; for he will not speak on his own, but will speak whatever he hears, and he will declare to you the things that are to come.

JOHN 16:13, NRSV

Reflection for leaders

It will be noticed that neither of the two readings for the festival of Trinity Sunday explicitly mentions the Trinity. That is because the notion of three persons in one God, equal yet distinct, one unit but each component different, is not spelt out anywhere in the Bible. The idea of the Trinity is instead a human response to the teaching of Jesus about the Father who sent him, the Son, and about the Spirit that was going to follow after him. The Trinity represents our way of trying to describe three aspects of a divine being, usually with a different saving purpose attributed to each: creation to the Father, redemption to the Son and sanctification to the Spirit. However, it is important to remember that, although they are distinct as persons, they do not act in isolation from the other two persons of the Trinity.

The relationship between Father, Son and Holy Spirit, each fully and equally God, yet not three but one, is a mystery to the human understanding. How, then, to explain it to children? Many different metaphors have been used in an attempt to make this difficult concept comprehensible: the three colours of a flag, the leaves on a clover or shamrock... All fall short, as any human comparison will do, but perhaps musical notes can help to demonstrate how three distinct components can make up one concept—in this case the sound made by a chord, or the notes in a tune. Each note has its own integrity, but together they can form a chord that is richer and deeper than a single note. Or one note has a particular sound, that when joined to other notes can produce a melody, separate components forming a greater whole.

This idea can be expanded to cover living in a good relationship with each other and in the church community. We need each other to form a family, a group or a community. We are all different and we all bring different gifts, just as different notes bring different sounds. Together we make a distinct and beautiful tune.

Bible story

After Jesus rose from the dead, his disciples saw him many times and in many different places. Jesus taught them more about God. 'Stay in Jerusalem,' he told them. 'Wait there, because I will send the Holy Spirit to you. Then go and tell people everywhere about me. Teach them everything I have done and said. I promise that I will always be there to help you.'

The apostles had often heard Jesus talk about the Holy Spirit, and how he would come to be with them after Jesus had gone.

'I wonder...'

I wonder what the disciples thought when they saw Jesus alive...

I wonder how the disciples felt as they waited for the Holy Spirit...

I wonder how we are all the same...

I wonder how we are all different...

I wonder how we can work together better...

Prayer activity

For Trinity Sunday, we are using the metaphor of music and musical notes: each note is different and distinct, yet when played together in a chord or tune they become something new and whole. Within the church building this will relate to anything to do with music. Encourage the children to explore the church and identify all the different things that can make music—the organ, a piano or keyboard, guitars or drum sets, not forgetting hymn books to remind us of the music of the human voice.

Sing a simple round, for example the chorus to 'Seek ye first the kingdom of God'. Encourage the children to notice that, although they are singing at a different time, it is the same words and the same tune. Let them experience how the words and the music work together to produce a tune, and how, although they have a different job to do within the song, it is only when they are all together that it sounds truly right. Help them to realise also that every song needs a singer, and that in order to sing together, each singer must listen to the sounds made by everyone else. So the love of God, Father, Son and Holy Spirit, works within all of us to form a beautiful whole—but we need to live out that love in order for it to be witnessed.

Sing the song again, telling the children to listen closely to each other and to themselves. At the end, allow a time of silence as the sound dies away.

If you have bells in your church, try to arrange for the children to hear them. Discuss the purpose of the bells—to call people to worship. Talk about the way that the bells remind not just people in church, but people in the wider community that they are being called to prayer. Help them to think about the people all over the world who are gathering together to pray, separate from the children, but one in worshipping God together.

Craft activities

Musical hands

This craft activity brings both our physical bodies and our voices together to make a musical pattern.

You will need:
- 1 length of paper, as long as you can easily cope with (a length of lining paper used in wallpapering is excellent for this craft)
- Black tape or a black marking pen (I used electrical insulating tape because it is easier than drawing lines, but if you have the skills, use a pen)
- Finger paints in a variety of colours (specially designed paint pads are easiest and cleanest to use, but poster paint poured into shallow dishes will do just as well)
- Soap, water and towels for washing hands afterwards

On the long sheet of paper mark out a five-line stave, either with black tape or with a pen.

Using the children's handprints, print musical 'notes' on the stave. You can print out a tune, if you mark out where the notes are to go beforehand.

If you like, you can print a quote from Psalm 150, for example, beneath the stave.

Making musical instruments

All sorts of musical instruments can be made very easily using the most basic household junk and a bit of tape! These ideas are just for starters. Don't forget bottles filled with different amounts of water that can be arranged to make a scale, or learning to whistle, clapping rhythms...

Shaker

You will need:
- Yoghurt pots, polystyrene or paper cups
- Strong sticky tape
- Stickers and paint to decorate
- Dried macaroni, rice or lentils

Put a small quantity of dried macaroni, rice or lentils in one of the containers.

Put another container upside down on top of the first and tape the two together.

Decorate with paint or stickers.

If you are working with young children, you might like to tape the two containers together prior to the activity.

Experiment with different types of filling to see what different sounds you can make—smaller or larger bits of macaroni, for example.

Drum

You will need:
- Empty tin cans, the larger the better (the sort that are opened with a ring pull, not a conventional tin opener, as these can produce sharp jagged edges)
- Balloon
- Masking tape
- Strong sticky tape
- Stickers or acrylic paint to decorate

Cut the end off the balloon and then stretch it over the top of the tin can.

Tape in place and decorate.

If you are working with young children, you might like to tape the balloon over the can prior to the activity, as uninflated balloons can be a safety hazard. Alternatively, if the tin can is very large, taping over the top with strips of masking tape is easier than using a balloon and quite a lot more robust.

Edible craft activities

Savoury musical stave

You will need (per child):
- 1 tortilla
- 5 or 6 cheese strings
- Carrot sticks or olives
- Celery

On the tortilla, lay out the five cheese strings horizontally, leaving a gap of about 1 cm between each string.

If you like, you can form the sixth cheese string into a treble or base clef and put it at the left-hand side of the stave.

Slice the carrots and place as notes on the stave. Alternatively, you can use olives as notes.

Slice the celery lengthways and use this to form the tails of the notes.

Sweet piano keyboard cakes

You will need (per child):
- 1 fairy cake
- 1 quantity of white fondant icing
- 1 quantity of black fondant icing
- Coloured icing or writing icing

Cut a circle of white fondant icing the same size as the top of the fairy cake.

With a knife, etch a horizontal line about one-third across the circle.

Using the knife, etch a number of lines vertically down from the horizontal line. These will be the white piano keys, so they need to be about 1–1.5 cm wide.

With the black fondant icing, make a number of small rectangles to form the black piano keys. Make sure they are small enough to allow some white to show beneath.

Place the black rectangles vertically in groups of two and three on the fairy cake, starting at the horizontal line.

Decorate the white icing above the horizontal line with flowers or patterns to make the lid of the keyboard.

*

Petertide

Theme: community

Place/object within the church building: church
building itself

Suggested Bible passages

Old Testament: Isaiah 51:1–6

Listen to me, you that pursue righteousness, you that see
the Lord. Look to the rock from which you were hewn, and
to the quarry from which you were dug.
ISAIAH 51:1

New Testament: Matthew 16:13–20

And I tell you, you are Peter, and on this rock I will build
my church, and the gates of Hades will not prevail against
it.
MATTHEW 16:18

Reflection for leaders

One Christmas, we decided that our children's service
would focus on the sheep belonging to the shepherds who

came to visit the infant Jesus. As part of the preparations I asked members of the congregation if they would knit some small sheep so that every child could be given one during the service. I gave them a pattern, lent out pairs of knitting needles and directed people in need of knitting advice towards some experts in that field. The congregation responded magnificently and very soon we had over 150 tiny knitted sheep, waiting to be given out in mid December.

As I looked at the baskets of woolly offerings, I realised that although everyone had been given the same knitting pattern, every single sheep was different. They were all recognisably sheep, but no two were alike: some were larger, as they had been knitted on bigger needles, some were much smaller, as the knitter's tension had been so tight. There were black sheep and white ones, brown and flecked and we even had one pink sheep. And it came to my mind that the sheep were in fact just like their manufacturers—all human beings, made in God's image, all seeking God, but all in their different ways, with different characters and lives. I realised that just as the basket of sheep was made more interesting by the variety within it, so our church community was made infinitely richer by the wealth of difference contained within its walls.

At Petertide we celebrate the action of Jesus in naming Peter as the one who would build up Christ's community on earth. Peter realised that God was acting through Jesus and that he truly was the Messiah, and the Church today exists because of Peter's faith and his determination to continue to believe and trust even when dangers and difficulties constantly surrounded him. Yet despite the fact that Jesus chose Peter above all others to continue his work on earth, Peter was a deeply flawed man. It was Peter who tried to walk on water like Jesus and fell in. It was Peter who misunderstood the moment of the transfiguration and wanted to build a shelter on the mountaintop, so that they could all stay there. And it was Peter who, when it came to the crunch, lost his nerve and denied Jesus. It is this very fragile, all too human person who was called a rock, and the Church that he built was promised that it would not be overcome.

The Church is a gift from God, and we must celebrate that gift. We must remember that God works through all of us—indeed it takes all of us, with our differences and our peculiarities, to enable the whole breadth and imagination of God's creation to be revealed through us. Church buildings in this part of the world are built of stone, of brick, of rock. They symbolise security, eternity, permanence. The buildings demonstrate some of the most amazing skills possessed by human beings, who created vast vaulted ceilings, beautiful windows, magnificent works of art so that all might worship the Creator. But it is within the hearts of the fragile community contained inside the building that the true work of worship is completed.

Bible story

Now when Jesus came into the district of Caesarea Philippi, he asked his disciples, 'Who do people say that the Son of Man is?' And they said, 'Some say John the Baptist, but others Elijah, and still others Jeremiah or one of the prophets.' He said to them, 'But who do you say that I am?' Simon Peter answered, 'You are the Messiah, the Son of the living God.' And Jesus answered him, 'Blessed are you, Simon son of Jonah! For flesh and blood has not revealed this to you, but my Father in heaven. And I tell you, you are Peter, and on this rock I will build my church, and the gates of Hades will not prevail against it. I will give you the keys of the kingdom of heaven, and whatever you bind on earth will be bound in heaven, and whatever you loose on earth will be loosed in heaven.' Then he sternly ordered the disciples not to tell anyone that he was the Messiah (Matthew 16:13–20).

'I wonder...'

I wonder how Peter felt when he recognised who Jesus was…
I wonder what Jesus saw in Peter…
I wonder what Peter thought when Jesus told him he would be the founder of the Church…
I wonder what the other disciples felt…
I wonder what Peter did next…

Prayer activity

You will need:
- Collection of stones
- Basket or container
- 4 candles

The stones can be gathered from the churchyard or garden (make sure they are clean) or bought from a garden centre. Be careful not to buy the polished pebbles, but ordinary rough stones.

Place one candle near the church door and one on the altar. Place the other two in the prayer circle. Place the stones in the basket in the middle of the prayer circle.

Explain that at the top of a mountain or along isolated tracks, there will often be placed at intervals large piles of rocks, called cairns. These can mark the summit of a mountain or indicate a path across stony or barren terrain, across glaciers, or a route that is difficult to navigate. In addition, cairns are used to commemorate events, from battle sites to places of injury or even memorial sites. These cairns can be small piles of stones or huge, carefully constructed hills.

The stones in the basket are not smooth, round stones, as might be expected. They are rough and uneven. They have been deliberately chosen like that. Firstly, they are rough because you cannot build a good cairn with smooth stones, which slide about and fall down. Secondly, they have been chosen because they are all different, scraped in places, with pieces chipped off. That is because they are representing people's lives, which are not all smooth and easygoing. There are difficult and sad parts. Just as the rough bits of a stone are what make it so individual, so all the parts of our lives make up who we are.

There is a very famous cairn on a pilgrimage route in Spain. A pilgrimage is a holy journey that people make to churches or other holy places, and thousands of people travel along the Camino de Santiago each year. About halfway along is a huge cairn, which gets bigger every year, built around the foot of an iron cross. The cairn gets bigger because every pilgrim who passes by adds a stone to the cairn. They do this to mark a stage on their journey, and as a visible sign that they were there. This is what we are going to do now. We are going to go on a journey round the church building, praying for the people who have worshipped here in the past, and all the people who will worship here in the future.

As you light one of the candles in the prayer circle, ask for a few moments' silence, then pray for all the people who have started their Christian journey in the church, for adults and children who have been baptised there, for Sunday schools and confirmation classes.

Walk the children around the outer edge of the church. Pause when you arrive at the altar and light the next candle. After a moment's silence pray for all the people who have worshipped in the church in the past, and for those who will follow after.

Continue walking in a circle. At the front door, light the third candle and pray for the community as it goes out beyond the walls of the church, and tries to lead a Christian life.

On returning to the prayer circle, invite everyone to take a stone and hold it in their hands, warming it. Ask them to pray for themselves and each other in silence.

Build the stones into a cairn shape and light the last candle in the prayer circle. Pray that each person may be like a living stone, strong in faith and supporting each other so that the church can continue to grow and flourish through them.

Craft activities

Church building

- 1 roll of lining paper
- Brick-shaped pieces of stiff paper or thin card
- Black marker pen
- Drinking straws
- Washable PVA glue

- 1 fairly large paintbrush for each colour paint
- Foam letters (optional)
- Poster paints in a variety of stone or brick colours
  (depending on the construction of your church: a
  brick building will need reds, terracottas, oranges
  and light browns; a stone building, black, grey
  and white)

Preparation

It is best to do a bit of experimenting beforehand with the consistency of the paints, adding water if necessary. They need to be runny enough to blow, but not so runny that they go all over the place.

With the black marker pen, draw the outline of your church on the lining paper. Make it as big as you can, sticking two pieces of paper together if you need to. It does not have to be an exact copy of your church, but if you can make it similar, that would be good.

Give the children a brick-shaped piece of paper each and ask them to write their names on them, using the black marker pen. This should not be washable, or the paint will make it run, so make sure the children are carefully supervised.

Give each child a drinking straw. Put blobs of different coloured paint on to the bricks and then blow the blobs so that the paint runs in all directions.

When the bricks are dry, glue them on to your church building.

You could write 'Our church' or the name of your church across the top, or use foam letters.

Milk carton church

You will need (per child):
- 1 large and 1 small empty milk carton, with the pouring spout (if there is one) removed
- Thin white or grey card or paper
- Slightly thicker darker grey card
- Crayons or felt pens
- Washable PVA glue
- Coloured paper
- Scissors

Cover the two milk cartons individually with white or grey paper and fasten with glue.

Glue the two cartons together to form a church and a steeple.

Measure two pieces of grey card that when folded in two will make a roof for the church building and steeple.

Draw squares or wavy lines on the grey card to look like roofing tiles.

While the church and steeple are drying, you can draw and cut out windows and doors from the coloured paper. Alternatively, you can draw these directly on to your building, but only after the glue has dried.

Edible craft activities

Savoury church building

You will need (per child):
- 4 slices of bread
- Margarine, paste or Marmite
- Slices of ham
- 1 slice of salami
- Cocktail sticks (optional)
- Knife for cutting

Spread the bread with the margarine or similar, and layer them on top of each other. Do not press down too hard as this presses the bread out of shape.

Cut the crusts from the bread.

Cut the bread layers about one third along, to form an oblong about 5 cm wide.

This will be the body of the church.

Cut the remaining section of the bread layers in half.

Stand one of these halves upright as the tower, and put it right against the church building. It helps if you fasten these together with a cocktail stick, but if the children are very young, this may be a health and safety hazard.

Cut the remaining section in half so that you have two squares of layered bread.

Take one of the sections apart and cut gradually bigger slices from each layer, so that you have a set of four 'steps'. Pile these on top of each other, then place on top of the tower as a roof.

Cut window shapes out of the ham, and a door shape out of the salami.

Sweet church building

You will need (per child):
- 1 slab of fruit cake (fruit cake is best for this craft as it is solid and can support itself, unlike sponge)
- Cocktail stick (optional)
- 2 oblong pieces of milk or dark chocolate
- Writing icing
- 3 American hard gum sweets for stained glass windows (optional)

Preparation for stained glass windows

Place the three American hard gums a little distance apart from each other on a piece of baking paper and microwave on medium for 20 seconds at a time until they can be rolled out with a rolling pin.

Roll out the sweets using another piece of baking paper on top, until they are flat.

If you want a stained glass effect, use different coloured sweets that will fuse together.

Cut two oblongs from the slab of cake. It is difficult to give precise measurements as cakes vary in size and shape, but you need to be able to stand one up against the other to act as church and tower.

Fasten these together with a cocktail stick if the children are old enough, bearing in mind the health and safety aspect.

Cut a square from the remaining fruit cake and then carve it into a square-based pyramid shape. This requires quite a sharp knife, and younger children may need this done for them beforehand.

Place the pyramid on top of the tower as the roof.

Use the chocolate as doors.

Cut window shapes from the rolled-out hard gums using scissors and stick to the cake with a small amount of writing icing.

*

St Michael and All Angels

Theme: angels

Place/object within the church building: representations of angels

Suggested Bible passages

Old Testament: Daniel 8:15–18

And I heard a human voice by the Ulai, calling, 'Gabriel, help this man understand the vision.'

DANIEL 8:16

New Testament: Revelation 12:7–13

And war broke out in heaven; Michael and his angels fought against the dragon. The dragon and his angels fought back, but they were defeated and there was no longer any place for them in heaven.

REVELATION 12:7–8

Reflection for leaders

Since the advent of such films as The Lord of the Rings, the Star Wars and Harry Potter series, we have become quite used to the concept of huge battles during which the fate of the entire world is decided. The forces of good and evil are regularly lined up against each other in all sorts of arrangements. Today's festival of St Michael and All Angels, however, celebrates that first, full and final victory over the forces of evil. The book of Revelation tells the story of that original battle where Satan was ejected from heaven, to God's eternal glory and Satan's eternal defeat. God has triumphed, in and through his Son Jesus Christ and the Holy Spirit, and although events on earth clearly indicate that the consequences of that triumph have not reached their fulfilment, there is no doubt that the war has been won.

This story, and the message that it brings, stands sharply contrasted to the popular notions of angels that abound today. The angels in the Bible are not designed to bring a personalised comfort or safety net to ease the journey of private individuals through this troubled world. Angels are agents of God; they carry out his bidding, and they are to be found throughout the Bible, in all sorts of contexts. An angel with a fiery sword guards the garden of Eden, and an angel tells Abraham that he will have a son, and later saves this son, Isaac, from being sacrificed. Angels are seen by the prophets, by a donkey, by Daniel. In the New Testament, angels surround Christ at his birth, spreading the news of the world's salvation to all who will hear it. After Christ's death, they announce the message of his resurrection.

The Feast of St Michael and All Angels celebrates the

eternal and total victory of good over evil, the beginning of a new era, a new world, God's kingdom come. It reminds us that God's power does not merely extend over this earth but over all of creation, the entire cosmos, and that we know only a tiny part of everything that is happening. The greatness of God is truly beyond our imagining. It also reminds us that this eternity, this power, this force for pure goodness, has broken into our world continually since its creation, and continues to do so. The existence of angels, messengers of God, shows us that God cares so intensely for every one of us that he is prepared to act directly, to intervene patiently, continuously and with immense love, constantly reinforcing the message of love that has been brought to us by his only Son.

Bible story

And war broke out in heaven; Michael and his angels fought against the dragon. The dragon and his angels fought back, but they were defeated, and there was no longer any place for them in heaven. The great dragon was thrown down, that ancient serpent, who is called the Devil and Satan, the deceiver of the whole world—he was thrown down to the earth, and his angels were thrown down with him (Revelation 12:7–9).

'I wonder…'

I wonder what a battle in heaven is like…
I wonder what Michael looks like…

I wonder what happened after Satan was defeated...
I wonder how I can fight evil...
I wonder how God feels about evil...

Prayer activity

You will need:
- Simple angel outlines, 1 for each child
- Felt-tip pens or crayons

Prior to this activity you need to tour your church looking for examples of angels. They may be found in wood carvings, stained glass windows or on memorials. If you can, find at least four. If you have no angels, find pictures of angels, if possible in completely different designs and styles, using different mediums.

Gather the children into a prayer circle. Explain that at the feast of St Michael and All Angels we celebrate not only the triumph of St Michael over the forces of evil for all time but all angels. Explain that you are going to look at some of the different ways angels have appeared to human beings in the Bible.

Take the children on a tour of the church, stopping at each of the four angels you have selected.

- Angel 1: Angels visit Abraham. Tell the story of the angelic visitors to Abraham and his wife Sarah. Even though Sarah was quite old, the angels told her she and Abraham would have a baby and that this baby's descendants would become as numerous as the stars in heaven (see Genesis 18:1–15).

- Angel 2: Angels walk with Moses. After the children of Israel had escaped from Egypt, led by Moses, they wandered in the desert for many years. They were accompanied on their journey by an angel (see, for example, Exodus 14:19–20).
- Angel 3: Gabriel tells Mary that she is going to have a baby who will be the Saviour of the world. When Jesus is born, news of his arrival is announced to the world by hosts of angels (see Luke 1:26–38).
- Angel 4: After Jesus' death, angels protect his followers as they seek to spread the good news of his love to all people (see, for example, Acts 5:19–20).

Return to the prayer circle. Give each child an angel. Explain that very often angels are messengers and that they are taking messages from God to his people. Give the example of Gabriel to Mary and the angels to the shepherds, as these will be most familiar to the children. Ask the children to imagine that they too are messengers from God. What message would they like to give to the world? Would it be that Jesus loves them? Would it be to ask them to stop fighting each other? Allow as much time as needed, then ask them to draw or write this message on the angel outline. Holding the angels, spend some time in silence, then thank God for his angels and the wonderful messages they bring.

Craft activities

Angel picture

- 1 length of black paper, as large as possible
- Silver foil or foam stars (you could get them in the sale at craft shops after Christmas and keep them)
- Gold or silver paper
- Gold or silver paint (buying the paint containers that are designed for handprints helps to keep the mess down)
- Pink and brown coloured paper
- Felt pens or crayons
- Glue sticks

Prepare the sky for the angels, either by cutting out stars from the silver foil and sticking them all over the black paper, or by sticking on the foam stars.

Cut a triangle from the gold or silver paper, about 15 cm high. This will be the angel's body.

Glue the body on to the paper.

Cut a circle from the pink or brown coloured paper. You can give the angel's face some features with felt pens or crayons if you wish, or just leave them blank.

Stick the head in position.

Either side of the triangle, place two gold or silver handprints, with fingers closed together and pointing at an angle away from the angel's body.

Repeat as often as you have room and materials.

Peg angel

There are many different variations to this craft, depending on the materials you have available.

You will need (per child):
- 3 circles about 15 cm in diameter of white net, muslin or fine cloth (net curtaining is a cheap solution)
- 1 traditional wooden dolly peg
- 1 white pipe cleaner
- 1 silver or gold pipe cleaner
- Gold or silver card
- Washable PVA glue
- Scissors

Preparation

You will need to provide a template for the angel wings, and if the children are very young, it is easier to have some wings already cut out.

Cut a small hole in the centre of the three circles and push the dolly peg through all three of them up to its neck. If the holes are too big, it does not matter, but it is easier to manage if there is a close fit.

Wrap the white pipe cleaner as tightly as possible around the neck of the peg and the top two centimetres of the fabric circles, leaving two ends of pipe cleaner of about 4 cm each. This will form both the bodice and the arms of the angel, so make sure that the pipe cleaner gets a good grip on the fabric as well as the peg.

Cut the gold or silver pipe cleaner in half. Wrap one end around the dolly peg's head, then make a larger circle at the other end to create a halo. This can be quite fiddly and may need adult help.

Cut out some angel wings from the gold or silver card. Fasten to the back of the angel's bodice with glue. If you are generous with the glue, this will also provide extra adhesion for the bodice and the dress.

Edible craft activities

Savoury angel

You will need (per child):
- 1 tortilla
- Marmite (optional, depending on taste)
- 2 slices of bread
- Cookie cutter with crenulations or a flower-shaped cookie cutter (optional)
- Knife for cutting
- Circle of an icing nozzle (optional)
- Cheese slice (optional)
- Olive (optional)

Spread the tortilla with marmite to give a night sky, if required.

Cut the crusts from the bread, then cut one slice into a square.

Cut the square into a triangle by making two cuts from the bottom corners to the centre of the top. This triangle is the angel body.

From the two smaller triangles left over, the wings will be made.

Using the crenulated or flower cutter, you can cut crinkly edges to the bottom of the robe and wings if you wish.

Place the triangle body in the centre of the tortilla. Place the two wings at an angle either side of the body.

From the second slice of bread cut a circle for the head of the angel. If you use the bottom circle of an icing nozzle, that gives a good-sized circle.

Put the angel's head on its body.

With the cheese slice you can make a halo, decorations for the robe, or stars for the sky. You can also make features from the olive.

Sweet angel

You will need (per child):
- 1 mini fairy cake
- Pink fondant icing
- 1 mini meringue (most easily available in tubs from the supermarket)
- Black writing icing
- 1 tsp of vanilla buttercream icing
- Rice paper for wings
- 1 Cheerio®

Preparation

You can buy the paper cake cases for the mini fairy cakes from any supermarket. It is easier if you have some miniature fairy cake baking tins, but you can manage perfectly well baking them in the paper cases on a baking sheet. Remember that they will only take about 5–8 minutes to bake.

Make a small ball from the pink fondant icing to form the angel's head. Older children may want to give the angel features with black writing icing, but these can be quite difficult to do.

Push the angel head gently on to the tip of the meringue. This needs to be done carefully or both meringue and head will be crushed!

Place the meringue on top of the miniature fairy cake. You can fasten it in place with a small quantity of buttercream icing.

Draw some wings on the rice paper and cut them out. Stick them to the angel's back with buttercream icing.

Place the Cheerio® on top of the head as a halo.

*

Harvest

Suggested Bible passages

Old Testament: Joel 2:21–29

Do not be afraid, land of Judah; be glad and rejoice. Surely the Lord has done great things!

JOEL 2:21, NIV

New Testament: Matthew 6:25–33

Consider the lilies of the field, how they grow; they neither toil nor spin, yet I tell you, even Solomon in all his glory was not clothed like one of these.

MATTHEW 6:28B–29, NRSV

Reflection for leaders

It all begins with an apple. An ordinary object, yet one that contains infinite variety. Did you know, for example, that apples are a member of the rose family of plants along with pears, peaches, plums and cherries? That there are approximately 7500 varieties of apple grown around the world, and that the trees don't start bearing fruit until about eight to ten years after they have been planted? Were you aware that apples are fat, sodium and cholesterol free, contain about 80 calories and are approximately 25 per cent air, which is why they float?

Archaeologists have found evidence that humans have been enjoying apples since 6500BC. They were eaten from the wild in Neolithic times, but veteran Roman soldiers who settled in Britain started to cultivate them. St Augustine established orchards in monasteries, and the Normans continued apple cultivation after 1066. The Black Death and the Wars of the Roses led to a decline in apple cultivation, but with Henry VIII this was halted, and in the 16th and 17th centuries the huge orchards of Kent, Herefordshire and Worcestershire were established.

Why all these interesting but apparently irrelevant facts about apples? Because every now and then we need to stop and think very closely about some of the things that we take for granted, and apples are among the most common. Within this one piece of fruit, with us throughout the year, fresh from the tree, stored at low temperatures or delivered from overseas to our supermarket shelves, lies all the miracle of God's creation.

Everywhere we go we are surrounded by the most remarkable objects of nature, created for us as part of God's amazing world. Put a seed under a microscope and it turns into the most extraordinary shaped object, beautifully coloured, a tiny wonder. Eat an apple slowly with thought going into each bite, thinking about the taste and texture of each mouthful, marvelling at the differences in colour of the skin, the flesh. Examine the tiny seeds and consider that if planted, they will grow into a large tree which will slowly develop until the point where it can bear fruit similar to the one that is being eaten.

Harvest Festival is a chance to celebrate the extraordinary in the ordinary, the miracles of creation that we see every day but very often don't appreciate. But it is more than that. For God made the world not just for us to enjoy but for us to care for. As stewards of his miracles it is our role to see that they don't get abused, exploited or kept for just one small group of people. The offertory plate symbolises our relationship with God as one of grateful response to all that has been given to us. When we give gifts at harvest and at other times, we are doing no more than giving back to God what is already his, that we have taken and, hopefully, used wisely and appreciatively until the time comes to return it to its true owner.

Bible story

Jesus looked at the people around him. Some were poor; others were sad or anxious; some could not walk or see.

'Don't worry about the everyday matters of living,' Jesus said. 'Don't worry about what you will eat or drink, or what clothes you are going to wear. Look around you at the wild birds. They don't have huge stores of food. They rely on God to feed them. God cares about them; but he cares about you even more than he cares about the birds. You will not live longer by worrying about your life.

'As for worrying about clothes, look at the lilies that grow in the fields. They do not work or dress themselves, but God has made them beautiful.

'If you put God first, he will make sure that you have everything you need—and much more besides.'

'I wonder...'

I wonder what Jesus felt when he saw the sad people around him...
I wonder what the people were sad and anxious about...
I wonder how the people felt after Jesus had told them not to worry...
I wonder what I worry about most...
I wonder what I should do when I am worried...

Prayer activity

You will need:
- Enough apples of three or four different varieties for every child to have one slice of each variety, plus a few extra apples
- Chopping board and knife
- The church's offertory plate or collecting bag
- 1 piece of paper for each child
- Pencils or crayons
- Flip chart and pens (optional)

Choose apple types that taste very different, such as Granny Smith and Braeburn. Also try and choose one that is from a rare variety—even the supermarkets now stock these, although they cost a bit more. If you can, research a bit about the apple variety: where it comes from, where it grows. Try to make sure the apples all come from the country in which you live.

Display the apples in a basket.

Gather the children in the prayer circle and show them the display of apples. Talk to them about each different type of apple, giving some of the apple facts from the leaders' reflection if the children are old enough. Cut the apples into slices, one variety at a time. Give each child a slice of apple from the same variety and ask them to eat it very slowly, thinking about each bite, then give them another slice of a different variety, until they have tried three or four different types of apple. Those children who don't want to eat the apple slices can have a whole one and examine its outside very carefully.

Together, think of as many descriptive words as possible for each apple; its shape, colour and texture.

Think about the different taste of each apple and try to think of words to describe it. If you wish, you can write all these words on a flip chart, until the paper is covered with different words, all describing one simple apple.

When the eating is over, ask the children to reflect on the amazing nature of the apples—how different they all are, how they taste. Explain that apples are a part of God's creation and that each tiny part is filled with the same wonderful variety as the apples. Explain that harvest is a time for looking closely at the wonderful world we live in and thanking God for it. It is also a time for remembering that we are responsible for caring for God's world, and for committing ourselves not to do things that might damage its future. Discuss with the children the sorts of things this might involve, such as not dropping litter or wasting water.

Ask each child to write or draw something to thank God for and place it in the offertory. Hold the bag for a short time of silence and reflection. End by saying a simple 'thank you' prayer.

Craft activities

Fruit and vegetable printing

You will need:
- A3 pieces of white or coloured paper
- 4 or 5 different coloured poster paints in shallow trays or plates.
- Potatoes, peppers, apples, mushrooms and/or pears
- Knife for cutting and carving

Preparation

You will need an even base to the plates for the paint, so don't use saucers as the paint coverage will not be even. Don't fill the plates too full as the paint just needs to cover the end surface of the vegetables. Better to tip a small amount of paint in and then keep refilling the plates or trays. It is a good idea to experiment with the consistency of the paint beforehand, as it is important that it is neither too sticky and thick nor too runny.

The A3 piece of paper needs to be quite stiff or it will wrinkle with the paint and pressure put upon it. Provide several sheets for each child so that they can experiment.

Cut the fruit and vegetables in half vertically, so that the shape and pattern of the inside is revealed. You may have to try two or three different vegetables with things like the peppers, as some of the insides are more effective than others. (Put the discarded vegetables aside for cooking later.)

Place the halved vegetables, cut side down, gently into the paint.

Make a vegetable print by pressing the painted side firmly on to the paper.

If you have older children, you can cut shapes from the potato halves—this is made easier if you use the tools sold for pumpkin carving.

The vegetables look very effective printed on to a plain sheet of paper, and for younger children that will be enough. Older children may want to paint a harvest basket or a landscape once they have experimented a bit, or create something totally different, such as a scarecrow, using the different vegetable shapes.

Salt dough fruit and vegetables

Salt dough is a staple of arts and crafts activities with children. It is easy and cheap to make, and can be used by all age groups.

The recipe for salt dough is very simple: you need plain white flour (the cheapest you can buy) mixed with half the amount each of water and salt. The salt used for dishwashers is cheapest. I usually make salt dough using a mug as a measure—half a mug of water and half a mug of salt mixed with a whole mug of flour. If you add about a teaspoon of oil for each mugful of flour, the dough will be smoother in consistency and easier to knead. You can add food colouring to the water to get different colours of dough.

Mix all the ingredients together until they form a kneadable dough. If it is too dry, add a bit more water, if too sticky, more flour.

You will need:
- 1 quantity of salt dough each in many different colours, including plain dough
- A rolling pin for each child
- Knives for cutting and shaping
- Different objects for making patterns, for example, cheese grater, lemon zester
- Paints
- Plastic basket from a 'pick your own' farm or similar
- Washable PVA glue if making a wreath

Mould the dough and form into different types of fruit and vegetables. You can use the knife and other kitchen objects for making surfaces and textures and adding details such as leaves and stalks.

When the fruit and vegetables have been made, put them to dry somewhere dry and warm, or cook very gently on a very low heat (about 100 degrees). This will take about an hour, more if the fruit is large. Alternatively, you can experiment by using a microwave on medium heat, initially for one minute, then in 20-second bursts.

When the fruit is dry, it can be painted and arranged in a basket.

Older children might like to plait a harvest wreath and put their fruit and vegetables on this. Roll out three long sausages of plain salt dough, then plait them together gently, making sure that the sausages keep their shape. Form into a circle and gently squash the ends together.

Make the size of the fruit and vegetables appropriate to the size of the wreath. Put them to dry separately, paint if required, then glue them on to the wreath with washable PVA glue.

Edible craft activities

Savoury scarecrow

You will need (per child):
- 2 slices of bread
- 1 slice of salami
- 1 tortilla chip
- Spaghetti cheese
- 2 Twiglets®
- Olive, red pepper
- Knife for cutting

Make the scarecrow's body first by cutting a body shape from the bread. You can provide a cardboard template if you like, or use a gingerbread man cookie cutter and cut off the hands, head and feet.

Put the salami slice on top of the body as the head, trimming as necessary to make the head in proportion to the body.

Place the tortilla chip on top of the head as a hat, then arrange some spaghetti cheese poking out from underneath the hat to form some straggly hair.

Break the Twiglets in half and place them at the ends of the jacket and trousers as arms and legs. You can place a whole

Twiglet under the body to look as if the scarecrow is put on a pole.

Tuck some more spaghetti cheese between the jacket and trousers and the arms and legs to look like straw poking out.

Give the scarecrow some features using cut bits of olive or other scraps from red peppers or similar.

Sweet scarecrow

You will need (per child):
- 1 syrup pancake
- Shredded wheat
- 1 black liquorice lace
- 2 blue Smarties®
- 2 wafer biscuits, either pink or brown
- Red liquorice lace
- Flower cake decorations (optional)

Place the syrup pancake on a plate as the scarecrow's face. Put one of the wafer biscuits horizontally across the top of the face to be the brim of the hat. Break or cut the second wafer biscuit so that it is a bit smaller than the first and place on top of the brim to be the crown of the hat. Decorate with red liquorice lace 'ribbon' and with flower cake decorations if you like.

Scrunch up some shredded wheat and arrange under the hat as straggly straw hair.

Two blue Smarties make the eyes, and the black liquorice lace the mouth. Break up small bits of lace to make the stitches going across the mouth.

*

All Saints

Suggested Bible passages

Old Testament: Psalm 16

As for the holy ones in the land, they are the noble in whom is all my delight.

PSALM 16:3

New Testament: Matthew 5:1–16

You are the light of the world.

MATTHEW 5:14A

Reflection for leaders

In the early years of the Church, to be a saint meant that you had died for your faith at a time when Christianity was forbidden and thousands of Christians were being killed for refusing to recant. Then Christianity became an accepted religion and persecution became rarer; the definition of a saint changed from one who had suffered death for God to

194

include those who had lived holy and extraordinary lives, often achieving great things in the name of Christ. Nowadays we have a history filled with an extraordinary number of saints who at first seem to have little in common with each other—and not much in common with ordinary people either! There is St Hugh, for example, a gifted administrator who had a pet swan. St Brigid is an abbess who converted the king of an unruly tribe with a cross of rushes picked from the floor. St Nicolas is known for his generous spirit, but he also rescued three boys from a pickle barrel, and St Margaret of Antioch slew a dragon... different saints with many different skills, but all characterised by one thing—a profound love for God and a deep desire to get to know him better. It is this love for God from which everything these saints said and did flowed, and towards which all their energies and gifts were channelled.

Nowadays, we tend to refer back to the New Testament meaning of saints that derives from the word 'sanctus', translated as 'holy'. In the letters of Paul in particular, this word 'sanctus' is applied to everyone who believes in Jesus and who tries to live according to his word and follow his path. In both letters to the Corinthians, we are all called saints (see, for example, 1 Corinthians 1:2). In fact, the word is always used in the plural in the Bible—Psalm 16 refers to 'the saints who are in the earth' (v. 3, KJV) in whom God delights. Saints are in fact normal people, who differ only from the rest of the world because of their desire to follow Christ and to share his love with those around them. In our church congregations we are surrounded by saints, all as different from each other in their character and attitudes, their habits and their lifestyle as those early saints who lived such extraordinary lives and did such extraordinary things.

We are united, uniquely, by our common purpose—to love God and to try to know him better. Through that purpose much that is wonderful is sure to come. We don't have to be great or wise or kill dragons to be a saint; we just have to be part of Christ's community.

In the traditional stained glass window of our church building we may see many wonderful stories of the brave and miraculous accomplishments of the saints and martyrs of our faith. Through them we see the love of God reflected in bright jewel-like colours, filling the church, making patterns upon the floor and furniture. So do their lives, marvellous and eccentric, give colour to our traditions and our prayers. We can also witness to the light that shines through plain glass windows, not as dramatic perhaps, but clear and pure, allowing the love of God to shine through.

Bible story

Paul wrote to the Christians in Corinth while he was in Ephesus.

'Every one of you is part of the body of Christ. God has given each one gifts to use for the good of everyone else. We all need each other. We suffer together and we are happy together. God has given us to each other so that his work can be done.'

'I wonder...'

I wonder what the people hearing this letter felt...
I wonder why Paul wrote this letter...

I wonder what a saint is...
I wonder what a saint does...
I wonder what makes me a saint...

Prayer activity

You will need:
- Large piece of card, with a simple outline of a person drawn upon it
- Small pieces of paper in different colours
- Glue

If your church has stained glass windows, take the children on a tour of the windows. If there are stories of the life of Jesus depicted, help them to guess which stories are referred to. If there are pictures of saints, tell them the stories of one or two of the saints and what they did. If you don't have stained glass windows, show the children a book of stained glass, highlighting the saints and telling some of their stories. Tell the children that not only the people in the windows, but all the people here in the church are also saints, because a saint is someone who tries to let the love of God shine through in their lives. The windows are in different colours because the saints all had different personalities and different gifts and skills, and all brought something different to their faith. They were held together by their love for God and by their constant efforts to share this with other people.

Bring the children back into the prayer circle and put the picture of the person in the middle, along with a basket of brightly coloured scraps of paper. Ask the children to create a mosaic person using the paper and glue. While they are doing this, talk to them about the different ways we can show our love for God. Ask them which of the saints seemed most interesting and what people would think if the same things happened today. Ask the children who they think the saints of today are.

When the picture is finished, remind them that we all show our love for God in different ways, but we are all held together by him and in him. Ask the children what the picture would look like if it were all one colour—not as interesting or attractive, surely! Then say that it is just as important to remember that the people with us are saints; that without them, our lives and our church would be much duller. Look at the picture and thank God for the examples of the lives of others.

Craft activities

Paper plate face

You will need (per child):
- 1 length of lining paper
- 1 paper plate
- Old magazines
- Brown, yellow and black wool
- Wobbly eyes
- Coloured paper and card
- Buttons
- Glue
- Scissors

This is a very simple craft that has the advantage of using

up scraps from other craft sessions. Using the paper plate as the face, you can cut out features from old magazines, or, more imaginatively, make button eyes, experiment with different textured paper and card for noses, and glue lengths of wool for hair. Add individual touches such as making hair ornaments, or braiding the wool to look like plaits. Decorate with sequinned earrings, or other piercings... perhaps even tattoos.

At the end of the craft activity, glue all the faces on to the lining paper. Use strong glue or a glue gun as they can be quite weighty.

Display your saints prominently in the church.

Stained glass saint picture

You will need:
- Colouring pictures of saints (from the internet; ideally, with quite simple outlines clearly marked in dark ink)
- Cheap wax crayons
- Cotton wool balls
- Small amount of cooking oil in a shallow dish
- Thin black card
- Scissors

Preparation

Draw the shape of a simple stained glass window on the black card—it need be no more than an arched window with perhaps three lines dividing it. Cut out the gaps between the lines so that you have the outline of a stained glass window.

Older children can design their own window, but cutting out without cutting through the lines can be quite difficult for smaller children.

Colour in the pictures of saints using the wax crayons. Experiment with colouring in very heavily and very lightly.

Once the picture is coloured in, turn it over. Take a cotton wool ball with a very small amount of cooking oil and lightly rub the back of the picture with the oil. Gradually the picture will become translucent. Leave the picture to dry.

Frame with the stained glass window outline.

Edible craft activities

Savoury saints

You will need (per child):
- 1 slice each of white and brown bread
- Person-shaped cookie cutter
- Knife for chopping and shaping
- Food for clothes—see below

Cut out the shape of two people from the bread with the cutter.

Decorate the people using some of the suggestions below. It depends on your imagination and the contents of your fridge!

- Eyes: olives or raisins for pupil with hard-boiled egg whites for the whites, cucumber, chorizo slices
- Hair and beards: cooked pasta curls, spaghetti string, shredded carrot, popcorn, broccoli

- Faces: salami, ham, cheese slice
- Nose: cherry tomato, slice of carrot, cucumber, celery
- Clothes: marmite or paste spread on, cheese slice or ham cut out
- Buttons: chorizo, raisins, olives

Sweet biscuit saints

You will need (per child):
- 2 or 3 biscuits made in the shape of a person
- Writing icing of different colours
- Mini Smarties®, chocolate buttons, liquorice laces, strawberry laces, fondant icing and/or Cheerios® (use odds and ends from other cooking activities to provide a good selection)
- Baking paper

Preparation

It is easy to find people cut-outs for the biscuits. If you like, you can make different male, female, girl and boy shapes. You could also swap 50 g of the flour for 50 g of cocoa powder in the biscuit dough, making a differently coloured biscuit person.

Design lots of different biscuit people. Use Cheerios or liquorice lace for hair, Smarties for buttons, or roll out fondant icing and design clothes.

Experiment with different facial expressions. Use the baking paper for trying out which work best; try angry, sad or happy faces.

✻

Remembrance

Theme: Remembrance

Place/object within the church building: memorials

Suggested Bible passages

Old Testament: Isaiah 40:27–31

Those who wait for the Lord shall renew their strength, they shall mount up with wings like eagles, they shall run and not be weary, they shall walk and not faint.
ISAIAH 40:31

New Testament: John 15:9–13

No one has greater love than this, to lay down one's life for one's friends.
JOHN 15:13

Reflection for leaders

The Imperial War Museum in London is a very impressive place to visit. It walks the difficult line between reporting the events of the war and evaluating them historically, expounding on the dangers and difficulties of armed combat, commending the individual and corporate acts of bravery and selflessness while at the same time giving the message that at all times the extinction of one human being by another should be viewed only as a last, terrible, resort. One recent exhibition that made a huge impression on me showed objects brought back from the recent conflict in Afghanistan by serving soldiers. There was, for example, a water carrier with two bullet holes in it—the soldier it belonged to did not realise he had come so close to death until he discovered the water had drained out from the carrier. There was a mug made from an ammunition shell, given insulation by a rough piece of cord wrapped around it; the label accompanying it told me that different patterns made by the cord indicated the ownership of the mug.

Two things struck me about this exhibition. Firstly, the huge tragedy of humankind, that we can make so much progress in some areas and so little in others. You only have to look at the World War I display elsewhere in the museum and the same young faces stare out at you from photographs, black and white but still uncanny in their resemblance to the ones on the landing upstairs. Even the souvenirs are the same—in the cabinets for 1915 can be found the same mugs fashioned from scraps of metal, and water bottles holed by bullets. One hundred years on and we are still at it. One hundred years on and our prayers for peace must continue, because we are not there yet.

The second thing to strike me was the importance of the individual. It is very easy when dealing with Remembrance Day to hear without absorbing the statistics of warfare—thousands killed or injured, hundreds of thousands slaughtered. It is not until you hear the names, see the faces of those who died, that it really comes home to you. Very often it is the anonymity of killing that allows people to do terrible things to each other. That's why our small community memorials matter so much. That is why alongside the service at the Cenotaph in London, it is vital that acts of remembrance are carried out up and down the country, commemorating those individuals from each community, those husbands, brothers, sons whose deaths made the lives of others so empty.

Christianity is a religion that values the individual. Jesus called just twelve men to be his disciples; his ministry was carried out in sparsely populated rural areas. Time and again he turned aside from the demands of the masses to focus on the needs of the individual: the widow whose son had died, the blind man, the small child, the woman who was bleeding. Individuals matter, and individuals can do great things—and that is where we come in. We can stand and be counted at the war memorials outside and inside our churches. We can pray together for those who have lost loved ones in wars, and we can commit ourselves to working for peace, wherever we are, whatever we do, because that's where it starts.

Bible story

The night before Passover, Jesus and his disciples met in the upstairs room to have supper together. Jesus knew that his time with his friends was drawing to an end. There was still so much he wanted to teach them.

Jesus wrapped a towel around his waist and filled a basin with water. Then he started to wash his friends' feet. Normally a servant would wash the dust from their feet before they sat down to a meal. Jesus knew how strange it would seem to his friends that he was doing it now.

'I won't let you wash *my* feet,' said Peter, as Jesus prepared to do just that.

'Peter, if I don't wash your feet, you cannot be my friend.'

'Then don't just wash my feet—wash all of me!' said Peter.

'There's no need,' said Jesus. 'Only your feet are dirty.'

When Jesus had finished, he returned to the table with his disciples.

'Do you understand what I have just done?' Jesus asked them. 'I am your teacher, but I have just done the job of a servant. I want you to treat each other with that same love and respect. Follow my example.'

'I wonder...'

I wonder how the disciples felt when Jesus was talking to them...

I wonder if Jesus knew he was going to die when he said this...

I wonder how much Jesus loves us...

I wonder what laying down your life for your friends means...

I wonder how this could work in my life...

Prayer activity

You will need:
- 1 A3 size piece of white card
- 6 bowls
- Glue

Per child:

- Each child will need:
- Outline of a four-petalled poppy, with a centre about the size of a 10p piece, cut out of white card
- 4 red paper petals that fit in the poppy outline
- 1 black centre circle
- Black pen or crayon
- Gold pen if possible (if not available, make the centre circle white)

Place six bowls with each of the components in the centre of the prayer circle. Give each child a white poppy template. Explain that today you are going to think about all the people who have been affected by war, or who are still suffering from its effects.

Ask each child to take a petal from the first bowl. This is the petal for all those people who have died in wars. Hold the petal in silence for a while, then mark the petal with a cross and glue it into place on the template.

The second petal is for those families who have lost people they love in wars. After a short silence, mark the petal with a heart and glue into place.

The third petal is for all people who are forced to leave their homes in a conflict zone. After a short silence, draw the outline of a house on the petal and glue into place.

The fourth petal is for governments and people in power— all those who decide whether to go to war or not. After a time of silence, draw a dove, the sign of peace, on the petal and glue into place.

The centre of the poppy is for each one of us, that we try to make decisions that work for peace in our own lives. Spend some time discussing what this could mean—turning aside instead of hitting back, not saying a hurtful thing, trying to keep our temper, helping to stop other people arguing. After a time of silence, write your name on the centre and glue into place.

When all the poppies have been made, glue them on to the white card. Write a prayer for peace, or simply 'Peace' or 'Our Prayer for Peace' on the picture. If it is appropriate, lead the children to the war memorial and lay the picture at its foot. Say the well-known verse from the poem 'For the Fallen' by Laurence Binyon (1869–1943) together:

They shall grow not old as we that are left grow old:
Age shall not weary them, nor the years condemn.
At the going down of the sun and in the morning
we will remember them.
We will remember them.

Craft activities

Poppy field

You will need:
- 1 length of lining paper
- Sponges (cheap bath or kitchen sponges cut into circles are fine)
- Blue and green poster paint in shallow dishes
- Small craft sticks
- Red felt
- Small black beads or buttons
- Red and black paper
- Glue gun

- Strong washable PVA glue
- Scissors, pencil

Preparation

You may want to glue (with a glue gun if available) the small craft sticks together to form crosses.

First of all, draw a rolling horizon on the lining paper.

With the sponges, paint blue sky and green fields in the appropriate places. The sponges will give a mottled effect; do not try and make the colour solid as the effect is better if there is some white in between.

While the paint is drying, make the poppies. First, cut a circle of red felt about 8 cm in diameter. Then draw a simple spiral pattern on to the felt. Cut this out as smoothly as possible. Glue the outside edges of the spiral together, then gather it in gently to make a three-dimensional flower shape. Put a black bead or button in the centre. Alternatively, you can cut some poppies out of red paper, using a British Legion poppy as a template, and sticking a black button or black paper in the centre.

Once the lining paper and poppies are dry, glue the craft stick crosses in lines across the paper. Glue the poppies at the foot of the crosses.

Poppy wreath

You will need:
- Stiff green card
- Red and black tissue paper
- Green plastic-coated garden wire, thin enough to twist easily and to be cut with a pair of scissors (available from garden and DIY shops)
- Washable PVA glue
- Scissors

Preparation

From the stiff green card cut a circle about 30 cm in diameter.

From the centre of this circle, cut another circle about 24 cm in diameter, so that you have a green wreath shape.

For each poppy, cut five circles about 8 cm in diameter from the red tissue paper. Cut a 20 cm length of green wire. Lay the circles on top of each other. Hold the circles in the centre, pinching the tissue until you have all five tissue centres between your finger and thumb.

Wrap the wire around the tissue circles you have pinched together. Make sure you catch all five circles within the wire wrapping. Leave some of the wire unwrapped.

Make enough poppies to cover the cardboard wreath. When you have made enough, either glue the poppies on to the wreath or wrap the green wire stems completely around the wreath.

Edible craft activities

Savoury cross

You will need (per child):
- 1 slice of brown bread
- 1 slice of white bread
- 2 cherry tomatoes
- 1 olive
- Cross-shaped cookie cutter
- Knife for cutting

Cut the crusts from the brown bread.

Cut a cross shape from the white bread and place on the brown bread—you can help to fasten it in place with margarine.

Slice the cherry tomatoes so that you have four ends.

Arrange at the bottom of the cross in the shape of a poppy.

Slice the olive in two and place one half in the centre of the poppy.

Sweet poppy

You will need (per child):
- 1 digestive biscuit
- Cream cheese
- 2 strawberries
- 1 blueberry
- Knife for cutting and spreading

Spread the digestive biscuit with cream cheese.

Slice the strawberries vertically in half, then cut the ends off so that you have two flat slices from each strawberry.

Arrange the strawberry slices into a flower shape, with the pointed end of the strawberry facing into the centre.

Place the blueberry in the centre.

Alternatively:

Sweet cross

You will need (per child):
- Vanilla buttercream icing
- Green food colouring
- 1 large syrup pancake
- 1 biscuit made in the shape of a cross (cross-shaped cookie cutters can be found in Hobbycraft or ordered online)
- 5 strawberries
- 1 small flower cutter
- Black writing icing

Mix the green food colouring into half of the buttercream icing.

Spread the bottom half of the syrup pancake with the green icing and the top half with the plain icing.

Place the cross-shaped biscuit so that it lies half on the green icing and half on the plain icing.

Slice the strawberries and cut flower shapes from them.

Place the strawberry flowers at the foot of the cross.

Give the poppies a black centre using the writing icing.

If you wish, you can use fairy cakes instead of pancakes and stand the biscuit crosses upright in the cakes. If you have a lot of fairy cakes, this can look very impressive.

Christ the King

Theme: the kind of king Jesus was

Place/object within the church building: chairs

Suggested Bible passages

New Testament: Revelation 21:1–7

Then he said, 'It is done. I am the Alpha and the Omega, the beginning and the end. To the thirsty I will give water as a gift from the spring of the water of life. Those who conquer will inherit these things, and I will be their God and they will be my children.'

REVELATION 21:6–7

New Testament: John 18:33–37

Jesus answered, 'My kingdom is not from this world.'

JOHN 18:36A

Reflection for leaders

Christ the King is celebrated on the last Sunday of the Christian year. It is a fairly recently created event—Pope Pius XI designated it so in 1925 and it entered into the Anglican

Church in the 1960s as more and more churches used the same set of readings as a basis for preaching each Sunday. It is not clear why the Pope made this festival at that time, but it is supposed that it has something to do with the situation of the world in the 1920s. Mussolini had by then been leader of Italy for three years, Hitler had been out of jail for a year, the Depression had America in its grip, and this had far-reaching effects into Europe. Christ the King came about, in fact, because a reminder was needed that God was in charge. Despite the difficulties that the world was struggling with, evil had been defeated, and Christ was victorious. The festival is a reminder that the things on earth for which we struggle, over which we fight, for which we bend our principles and for which we cheat others, are not in fact what it's all about. We are reminded of a kingdom greater than any here on earth, a power that encompasses all this world has to offer and more—riches and wealth of a magnitude that is unimaginable. But it also reminds us that this kingdom, this power and these riches are not the same as the world offers. Jesus came into the world not as a mighty leader nor as a rich man—he was offered and rejected riches and power after 40 days and nights in the desert, before he began his ministry (see, for example, Matthew 4:1–11). Jesus came to show God's people a new way, a new set of principles, a way of living beyond the everyday.

The kingship of Christ has confused many, beginning with Herod, who saw in Jesus a rival, completely misunderstanding the nature of Jesus' kingship. Pontius Pilate could not recognise a king in the figure of the bloodied, beaten man who stood before him and refused to plead for his life. Both these rulers were using a different measure, the wrong measure, by which to judge kingship. Christ offered instead a kingdom of love, of peace, of sacrifice, one that brought healing, not destruction, transformation, not damage.

At Christ the King we celebrate the triumph of good over evil and look beyond the riches the world offers to those of heaven. We must also take care to see Christ working within each and every one of our community—which is the reason for the focus on the church chair or pew. Beside each one of us, every Sunday, sits a fellow citizen of heaven, a child of God, someone whom God loves with his whole heart, battered and flawed though that person might be. And if God loves them, who is so much a better judge than any of us can ever be, who are we not to?

Bible story

When John was an old man, he was sent to live in exile on the island of Patmos.

One day the Holy Spirit revealed strange things to John and told him to write them down on a scroll and send them to the Christians in Ephesus, Smyrna, Pergamum, Thyatira, Sardis, Philadelphia and Laodicea.

John looked to see who it was who was speaking to him and was amazed to see Jesus, not as he remembered him from when they worked together in Galilee but shining like the sun, God in all his glory.

The sight was so awesome that John fell at Jesus' feet. Then Jesus touched John's head gently and spoke:

'Do not be afraid, John,' he said. 'I am the first and the last, the living one. I was dead, but look, I am alive now and I will live for ever and ever.'

'I wonder…'

I wonder how John knew it was the Holy Spirit talking to him…
I wonder what John felt when he saw Jesus…
I wonder if John was pleased when he heard Jesus' words…
I wonder if Jesus speaks to us today…
I wonder what Jesus' words mean…

Prayer activity

You will need:
- Map of the world (you could buy this or print from the internet or draw out a rough map on a large piece of paper)
- Crown shapes (cut these out of thin card or buy readymade crown shapes from craft shops such as Hobbycraft)
- Felt pens
- Double-sided sticky tape

Place the map of the world in the middle of the prayer circle and explain that Christ the King celebrates the fact that Jesus rules over the whole earth. If the children are quite young, encourage them to name countries that they know, and find them on the map. Take it in turns to stick a crown shape on to the country they have found. Older children might benefit from a discussion around the fact that even though there are places in the world that are in conflict or trouble, Christians believe in the ultimate triumph of good over evil, and the feast of Christ the King is a symbol of that. Ask them to name some places in the world that are hazardous to live in, whether through natural disasters or conflict. Stick crown shapes over these countries, praying for those who live there.

Then discuss with the children how Christ the King celebrates the victory of Jesus not only in the world but in our hearts as well. In our daily lives we must try to put Jesus first in all the ordinary things we do.

Ask the children to walk slowly to a chair or a seat or a pew anywhere in the church. Ask them to sit there for a while in silence, then, without moving their heads, pray for any of the people they can see in front of them. Ask them to turn around and pray for the people they see behind them. Finally, they can pray for themselves, that they remember Jesus' presence in everything they do.

Craft activities

Papier mâché world

This is a very messy craft, so encourage the children to wear their oldest clothes.

The craft has to be left to dry out completely at one stage, so should be done on two separate occasions.

You will need (per child):
First session:
- 1 balloon
- Wallpaper paste
- Newspaper torn into long strips
- Lining paper torn into long strips

Second session:
- Blue, green and brown poster paints
- 1 large craft stick
- PVA glue
- Paintbrushes
- Sequins, sticky shapes, glitter and so on
- Felt pens

Preparation for first session

Mix the wallpaper paste to the correct consistency according to the instructions on the packet.

Preparation for second session

Mix the poster paints with some washable PVA glue.

Glue the craft sticks into a cross shape with a glue gun.

First session

Blow up the balloon until it is as spherical as possible.

On to one section of the balloon, paint some wallpaper paste.

Cover the paste with strips of newspaper, then paint some wallpaper paste on to another section of the balloon and cover that with strips of newspaper.

When the entire balloon has been covered with strips of newspaper, begin at the beginning again and add another layer of newspaper.

Continue for at least four layers.

The fifth layer should be smaller strips of lining paper. This is not so mouldable, so smaller pieces are needed. Use lining paper to get a smooth final surface to paint on. It is worth taking your time over this layer.

Leave to dry for at least three days, preferably in a warm place.

Second session

When the papier mâché is completely dried out, pop the balloon by inserting a knife and making a small slit in the papier mâché, no wider than a large craft stick.

Paint the papier mâché to look like the world. Pictures of a world map or a globe would be a useful guide. Otherwise, just patches of blue and green and brown will do.

While the world is drying, decorate the craft stick cross. Older children might like to write 'Christ the King' on the cross piece.

Carefully insert the cross into the gap in the papier mâché world. It might need glue or tape to hold it secure.

Crowns

You will need:
- Lengths of thin cardboard, about A3 size, long enough to wrap round a child's head
- Stapler
- Scissors
- Washable PVA glue
- Crayons or felt pens
- Sequins, stick-on shapes, foam shapes, scraps of coloured paper and any other decorations

Cut a length of card long enough to go around the child's head, plus about 3 cm overlap.

Draw a line down the crown to indicate which is the overlap area—this should not be decorated as it makes fastening together very tricky.

If you wish, you can cut the top of the crown in a zigzag, wavy line or other pattern.

Stick as many decorations on to the crown as possible.

It is best to leave the crown to dry while it is still flat, but if you can't wait, staple it together and wear carefully until the glue is dry!

Edible craft activities

Savoury crown

You will need (per child):
- 1 bagel
- Squirty cheese
- About 20 tortilla chips
- Knife
- Slices of cheese (optional)
- Small star or heart cutters (optional)

Slice the bagel in half.

Squirt a thick circle of cheese on to the bagel. The slower you go, the more comes out.

Gently press a circle of tortilla chips, points upward, into the squirty cheese, so that they look like the crenulations of a crown.

If you wish, you can decorate the rest of the crown with

shapes cut from cheese slices, using tiny cutters, if you have them, or freehand.

Sweet crown

You will need (per child):
- 1 ring doughnut, ideally glazed (they are sticky but not sugary—the sugar gets everywhere)
- 1 quantity of biscuit dough
- Vanilla buttercream icing
- Coloured writing icing
- Sugared balls, shapes and any other cake decorations, or small sweets
- Flower cookie cutter (optional)

Preparation

Make the biscuit dough into oblongs that are a bit longer than the doughnut is high—about 6 cm. They should be between 2.5 and 3 cm wide. You can cut the top of the biscuit into a point, using a triangle template, or cut a wavy line using the edge of a flower biscuit cutter.

First, determine how many biscuits are needed to go round the doughnut, by leaning them against the doughnut. If there is a gap, you can decide whether to risk breaking a biscuit in half, leaving a small gap between biscuits as you go round, or just putting the gap at the back.

Decorate the biscuits using writing icing, Smarties® and other cake decorations. It can look very effective if every biscuit is decorated in the same way.

Spread some buttercream icing gently but generously on to the edge of the doughnut.

Stick the biscuits on to the icing.

Also by Sally Welch

Edible Bible Crafts

64 delicious story-based craft ideas for children

If you're looking for child-friendly Bible-themed cooking activities, this is the book for you!

Sally Welch brings the Bible to life for 3–11s with her range of edible crafts, covering twelve Old Testament stories, twelve New Testament stories and eight key festivals from the church year. Each unit gives the Bible story in a children's version, a short reflection on the passage, and a sweet and a savoury recipe idea.

The recipes use readily available ingredients and equipment, require no cooking during the craft session and can be used in a variety of situations, including Sunday schools, midweek clubs and Messy Church events.

The book also includes detailed information about set-up and preparation, tips on where to buy ingredients, and basic recipes to form the basis of the crafts, such as fairy cakes, biscuits, pastry, together with egg- and gluten-free alternatives.

ISBN 978 0 85746 243 5   £11.99

Available from your local Christian bookshop or direct from BRF: www.brfonline.org.uk.

Enjoyed
this book?

Write a review—we'd love to hear what you think.
Email: reviews@brf.org.uk

Keep up to date—receive details of our new books as they happen.
Sign up for email news and select your interest groups at:
www.brfonline.org.uk/findoutmore/

Follow us on Twitter @brfonline

By post—to receive new title information by post (UK only), complete the form below and post to: BRF Mailing Lists, 15 The Chambers, Vineyard, Abingdon, Oxfordshire, OX14 3FE

Your Details	
Name _____	
Address_____	
_____	
Town/City _____	Post Code _____
Email _____	

Your Interest Groups (*Please tick as appropriate)	
☐ Advent/Lent	☐ Messy Church
☐ Bible Reading & Study	☐ Pastoral
☐ Children's Books	☐ Prayer & Spirituality
☐ Discipleship	☐ Resources for Children's Church
☐ Leadership	☐ Resources for Schools

Support your local bookshop
Ask about their new title information schemes.